The
Herbaceous Border

The Herbaceous Border

OLIVER DAWSON

David & Charles : Newton Abbot

ISBN 0 7153 6211 9

Set in 11/13 Baskerville
and printed in Great Britain
by W J Holman Limited Dawlish
for David & Charles (Holdings) Limited
South Devon House Newton Abbot Devon

Contents

List of Illustrations

DIAGRAMS

Photographs are reproduced by permission of the *Echo &* *Post*, Hemel Hempstead

Introduction

It is more than 100 years since herbaceous plants were first segregated to create a separate and distinct garden feature but it was not until Gertrude Jekyll and William Robinson, with their emphasis on natural plant groupings, came on the scene around the turn of the century that the herbaceous border came into its own as a popular form of gardening.

Both these distinguished gardeners were destined to have a profound influence on the design of gardens lasting from Victorian times right up to the present day. In his well known book, *The English Flower Garden,* in a chapter on 'Borders of Hardy Flowers', William Robinson wrote: 'There is nothing whatever used in bedding out to be compared with the many families of hardy plants.'

It was not long before a herbaceous border became the 'in' thing in every garden of any appreciable size. The owners of large suburban gardens were not slow to follow this new gardening fashion. In smaller gardens, however, the Victorian tradition of carpet bedding died hard and in the majority of small town and suburban gardens alyssum, lobelia and geraniums still retained their popularity until the years following World War II, when an upsurge of interest in gardening and the rise of the horticultural supermarket or garden centre brought the knowledge of many former specialists' plants to the amateur gardener.

Up to the middle thirties, the herbaceous border remained a dominant feature of almost every large garden of note. Until that time garden labour was still comparatively easy to come

by. Even the owner of a modest suburban plot could afford
and what is more, obtain, the services of a jobbing gardener
on a day to day basis.

It was he who carried out most of the boring and backaching chores, such as digging, weeding of lawns and paths
and the maintenance work in the herbaceous border, leaving
the owner of the garden free to indulge in that pleasantest
of horticultural pastimes, pottering.

From 1910 to 1930 was the heyday of the herbaceous border. In the years immediately following World War II when
garden help, apart from the occasional odd job man—and
some of them could be very odd—was impossible to get, the
herbaceous border as Gertrude Jekyll knew it practically disappeared. Many, in any case, had already fallen victim to the
government's 'Dig for Victory' campaign and had been turned
over to fruit or vegetables. Others had become so weed infested as to be beyond all reasonable hope of restoration.

Hardy perennials were still as widely grown as ever but
now we were learning to use them in association with other
types of plant, with small shrubs, roses, spring bulbs, dahlias
and even alpine plants to extend the season of display.

This has done much to restore the herbaceous border, or
the mixed border, as it is more commonly referred to nowadays, to its former popularity. Other important labour saving
features of the present day border include the use of ground
cover plants to smother weeds and conserve soil moisture and
the employment of new types of perennials and new varieties
of old favourites that can stand up to the most blustery
weather without any need for staking or other forms of
support.

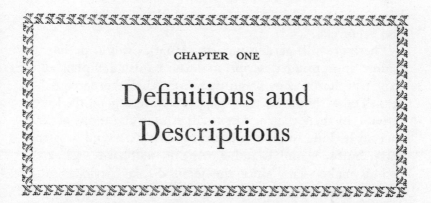

CHAPTER ONE

Definitions and Descriptions

In its original form the herbaceous border was a garden feature in which all the plants were hardy herbaceous perennials. This immediately begs the question of what is a hardy herbaceous perennial, a term normally shortened to hardy perennial. The best definition is 'a plant that loses its leaves at the end of the growing season and renews itself from the base the following year'.

Although this is an adequate description of the great majority of hardy perennials, there are, as always, numerous exceptions. One of these is the popular bergenia, formerly known as megasea. The bergenias retain their large fleshy leaves in winter and are very showy in their crimson winter livery.

Another is *Acanthus mollis*—Bear's Breeches—whose handsome bottle-green foliage provides welcome winter interest in the border.

Others, the in-betweens of the plant world, display some of the characteristics of shrubs in retaining woody growth above ground from which new leaves emerge in spring. These are sometimes known as sub-shrubs although they possess more of the characteristics of hardy perennials than of shrubs. Typical examples are the plumbago, *Ceratostigma willmottiae* and the South African Cape figwort, *Phygelia capensis*. The

11

latter, which has vivid scarlet tubular flowers in summer, is also evergreen.

There are still garden purists—fanatics would perhaps be a more appropriate description—who banish any plant other than true herbaceous perennials from their herbaceous borders. Today, however, most gardeners are a good deal more catholic in their choice. They will stretch the terms of reference to include roses, small shrubs such as lavender or rosemary, bulbs, biennials and hardy and half-hardy annuals.

This makes sense since the main display period of most hardy perennials comes between April and September, leaving a herbaceous border proper dull and uninteresting for the remaining half of the year. The inclusion of other kinds of plants extends the season of display considerably in addition to providing a greater diversity of interest.

This last point is of particular importance in the smaller present-day gardens. Every inch of space must be made to yield its full quota of interest over as long a period as possible. In the pages that follow, therefore, the term border should be read as referring to this latter type of garden feature where plants other than actual herbaceous perennials, are allowed to live in happy association.

One of the greatest virtues of hardy perennials is their versatility and variety of forms, flower and texture. They range in height from eight-footers such as hollyhocks, delphiniums and verbascums down to the lowliest dwarf carpeters like the cultivated deadnettles and the woolly-leaved lambs' ears, *Stachys lanata*.

And what could offer greater contrasts than the petal-packed globular blooms of herbaceous peonies and the tall spikes of lupins and delphiniums, or more differing textures than the dark polished foliage of acanthus and the lacy filigree of the meadow rue?

Perennials are equally noteworthy for their adaptability to a wide variety of uses. Some flourish best in hot sandy soils;

others have a preference for partial shade. There are even those, like the lovely water irises and bog primulas, that actually prefer to paddle, root-deep in waterlogged soil.

PLANNING AND PLANTING

Before starting on the planning and planting of a herbaceous border, it is advisable to get to know the characteristics and, if possible, the vital statistics relating to height and spread, of the subjects to be used. This objective is most easily achieved by observing them in growth in parks and other municipal or public gardens, by visits to other people's gardens and by expeditions to nurseries and garden centres at different times of the year.

It is easy enough to have a 'riot of colour' in the border from June right through to September. What *is* more difficult is the ability to furnish it with plants that will provide interest earlier and later in the year. Since most herbaceous perennials die back to ground level in winter and do not start into active top growth again until April, this might appear to pose a difficult problem.

There are, however, quite a few hardy perennials that come into bloom in March and April as well as others whose foliage persists throughout the winter. These are described in detail in other chapters.

Drifts of tulips, daffodils, hyacinths and other spring-flowering bulbs, together with biennials such as wallflowers, sweet williams and Canterbury bells can be used as well to give colour and continuity until the main display gets underway. In winter, flowering shrubs such as witch hazel, daphnes, wintersweet and *Viburnum fragrans*, all of which are comparatively compact and slow growing will add a contribution of colour.

The newcomer to gardening would be well advised to consider the nucleus of hardy perennials that can be relied upon to give a first-class display in the widest variety of soils and situations. These, or some of them, should form the basis of any new border. More exotic or out of the ordinary kinds can always be tried when the border is on its way to becoming established.

Among the perennials that warrant inclusion in every planting scheme are lupins, delphiniums, peonies, phlox, oriental poppies, shasta daisies, anchusa, anthemis, rudbeckias, campanulas, heleniums, helianthus, salvias, scabious and goldenrod. These are all plants of medium to tall growth.

For the front of the border, there are columbines, pinks, geums, irises and catmint, all easy to grow and satisfactory in a wide variety of soil conditions. These two groups alone would be capable of providing a magnificent display but there are also hosts of other perennials, both popular and lesser known whose inclusion will be instrumental in giving the border that extra touch of style that separates it from the commonplace. Detailed descriptions of these appear in Chapter 7.

A few years ago, a sizeable specimen of any of the better-known border plants could be purchased very cheaply. Today, they are becoming progressively dearer so that stocking a border of any appreciable size completely in the first season can be an expensive project.

An alternative to buying the recommended three to six plants of each kind is to plant initially only one specimen of each, splitting up the resulting clumps into the required number of divisions in their second or third season.

This is practicable only with perennials that have a fairly rapid rate of increase and which do not resent disturbance. With subjects such as michaelmas daisies, phlox, heleniums, rudbeckias and the like it is not only possible but also advisable to split the clumps annually.

This procedure, however, would be extremely detrimental to other well-known border plants such as peonies, gypsophila and alstromerias. Once in position, these should stay where they are. Then they will increase in beauty with each successive season. Peonies, in particular, resent being disturbed and may sulk for some years before starting to produce flowers in any quantity again.

Some perennials, of which delphiniums are an example, are relatively short lived. Others, like peonies, will continue to flower and flourish in the same position for a lifetime or longer. In the case of the former kinds, it is advisable to raise fresh stocks of plants from seed or cuttings every other year or so. Many perennials are as easy to propagate from seed as annuals or biennials while stocks of many others can be increased by stem or root cuttings.

A herbaceous border need not remain a static garden feature. The mere fact that so many of its occupants need regular division and replanting makes it easy to regroup plants at frequent intervals and even, if desired, to change any colour schemes or groupings completely.

During the first and second season, a newly planted border is almost certain to contain many wide open spaces between individual plants and plant groupings. Such gaps can be filled temporarily with hardy and half-hardy annuals. In this connection, petunias, zinnias, French and African marigolds, larkspurs, stocks and tobacco plants are some of those that will make a valuable contribution.

Page 18   A group of bearded irises (*I. germanica*)

foliage a perfect backcloth for every kind of border plant. The two long parallel borders in the Royal Horticultural Society's gardens at Wisley, England, were a good example of its use for this purpose. Alas, the powers that be recently decreed that these two borders should be removed and grass now grows where yews and perennials formerly flourished. But there are many other outstanding examples in gardens open to the public. Although yew is both slow growing and expensive, there is no finer hedging shrub obtainable for those prepared to wait the six or more years that it takes a hedge of this kind to come to maturity. The initial cost is largely offset by the subsequent saving in labour. Yew hedges need only one annual trim to keep them neat and tidy.

Holly is another evergreen that makes a magnificent hedge. Its polished dark green foliage is especially attractive when each leaf reflects the sun's rays in winter. Holly is not quite as slow growing as yew: it puts on quite a rapid spurt after the second or third season. Like yew, it requires little attention when compared with such vigorous hedgers as privet or the shrubby honeysuckle, *Lonicera nitida,* both of which need clipping every few weeks during the growing season.

Holly and yew are not such blatant soil robbers as most other hedging plants. Next to these, for more rapid results, I would choose beech or hornbeam as much for the cheerful russet of their winter foliage as for the delicate apple green of their leaves in spring.

Both are quite fast growers; hornbeam, however, is the better choice for heavy, damp soils.

Lonicera nitida, with its close-packed glossy evergreen foliage makes a fine hedge that bears comparison with yew provided it is clipped regularly and is not allowed to grow more than five to six feet tall. Without regular attention, it has a tendency to become leggy and develop bare patches at its base. A newer variety, *L.n. fertilis* (syn *L. pileata yunnanensis*) is an improvement on the former in these respects.

B

Even the much maligned privet can make an excellent hedge if it is kept closely and regularly clipped. But I would hesitate to plant it as a background to perennials since it is such a gross feeder, with masses of fibrous roots that wander far afield in their search for nourishment. In one of my gardens, however, presented with a privet hedge as a *fait accompli,* I did manage to keep its roots in check by sinking old sheets of corrugated iron, edge on in the soil, about a foot from the base.

Flowering hedges, such as shrub roses, whose blooms tend to distract from the actual border display are to my mind unsuitable, but the golden blossoms of the evergreen *Berberis stenophylla,* a hedging shrub of outstanding beauty, will have made their exit by the time the early summer display begins. Another fine evergreen flowering shrub, particularly suitable for a really wide border is *Cotoneaster lacteus.* It has masses of creamy-white flowers in late spring that are followed by long-lasting scarlet berries to provide autumn and winter colour.

Since hard clipping inhibits their flowering, however, both these subjects are more suited to the informal kind of border where shrubs and perennials are grown together and where their arching habit of growth provides a more suitable background than that of a clipped formal hedge.

Conifer hedges remain an attractive feature of the garden the whole year through and make superb foils for the flower colours in summer. Many varieties of Lawson's cypress, *Chamaecyparis lawsoniana,* make excellent hedging subjects, including the blue-grey and golden forms, 'Allumii' and 'Stewartii'.

One of the best choices is the variety known as 'Green Hedger', with bright-green foliage and a rapid rate of growth. But the fastest of all hedging conifers is *Cupressocyparis leylandii,* a bigeneric hybrid, (*Cupressus macrocarpa* x *Chamaecyparis nootkanensis*). This, unlike its first parent, is perfectly hardy and will withstand the fiercest gales to make an excellent windbreak. It stands up well to clipping and will increase in height at the rate of 3ft annually.

Walls of mellow brick or stone make a perfect background for a herbaceous border. They can, however, in addition to the disadvantages already mentioned, prevent the free circulation of air among plants growing at the foot of them. In such situations, perennials susceptible to mildew, such as phlox and michaelmas daisies, may suffer severely.

DIMENSIONS OF THE BORDER

No hard and fast rules can be laid down as to the exact dimensions of a herbaceous border. It can vary in depth according to site, the purpose for which it is required (eg as a screen for a vegetable or fruit garden, as a frame for a stretch of lawn or as a boundary for one or both sides of the garden) A rough guide to depth is that it should be approximately twice the height of the tallest plants in the border.

As very few hardy perennials exceed 6ft in height, this will restrict the maximum depth to about 12ft. In the majority of newer gardens, it is unlikely that this could be exceeded in any case. It would, however, be unwise to settle for a depth of less than 5ft if a continuous and colourful display is desired.

These dimensions exclude the depth of any backing hedge. In the case of borders more than 8-10ft deep, it would be advisable to leave a service strip 2-3ft wide between any hedge, wall or fence and the plants in the back row. If the soil is heavy and inclined to pack down hard when walked on, stepping stones or continuous paving should be laid to allow access during spells of wet weather.

A double-sided border, often used at one time as an edging or screen for vegetables or fruit and an attractive feature abutting on a path or grass walk should not normally be wider than 6-7ft. Plant heights are graded with the tallest in the centre. One great advantage of this kind of border is that the beauty of the plants can be appreciated, in the round. Maintenance is easy. Where space permits, a border of this kind in the kitchen garden makes an ideal cutting bed for flowers for the house, since there is no need to rob the main border and detract from its display.

Many perennials cut and last well. Those with a flower arranger in the family will be helping themselves as well as her by providing a source of flowers she can snip without any feeling of guilt.

A more recent way of displaying perennials and one that is fast becoming very popular in view of its space-saving character, where small gardens are concerned, is the 'island' border. These are of irregular shape—kidney, elliptical and boomerang are three that come to mind—and, since they can be of any convenient size with a minimum width of around 4ft, they can be adapted to the needs of the small or irregularly shaped garden more easily than the more conventional long rectangle. Like the double-sided border, they offer better opportunities of viewing the plants—especially the taller kinds—in greater detail.

There should be room for several of these island borders in any garden of medium size so that each one can, if so desired, be restricted to certain types of plants or to particular colours, either of flowers or foliage. There is a border of this kind in my present garden in which only grey and silver-leaved perennials are grown with small shrubs of similar character, such as lavender, artemisia, helichrysum and senecio to keep them company.

PREPARATION OF SITE

Thorough preparation of the site for a herbaceous border is an operation that is all important for its continuing success. Much will depend on the use to which it has been put formerly. It will obviously be much easier to prepare for planting the site of a former lawn or vegetable garden than to tackle virgin pasture or neglected scrub. One of my hardest jobs, before the use of bulldozers became commonplace, was making a border in a clearing in a stretch of Surrey woodland.

The entire plot was a jungle, thick with tall brambles and 6ft saplings, undergrown with nettles, ground elder and coarse grasses. An over optimistic sales representative gave me a demonstration with several different makes of rotavator. After breaking the blades of two on partly rotted tree stumps, he had to admit defeat. There was no alternative but to clear the entire area by hand. This entailed winkling out every single briar and bramble root with a mattock before digging could begin in earnest.

The average border site is seldom as difficult to knock into shape as this. Where it is former turf or cultivated ground, it will be sufficient to dig it over to a depth of 1 1½ft. The turf, if of good quality, can be sliced off with a sharp spade or turfing iron. Some use can often be found for this in other parts of the garden for repairing or extending existing lawns.

Where this is not practicable, the turf should be placed face down in the trenches as digging proceeds. During the digging process, all perennial weeds must be removed and burnt. They should not go on the compost heap to start into growth afresh. Particularly insidious are weeds such as ground elder, dandelions, docks, bindweed and creeping buttercup.

Once any of these have got a hold in the border, it could be necessary to dig up and replant whole clumps or even to replant entire areas since they become intertwined with the roots of the perennials and cannot be dislodged without digging up the plants and shaking their roots free of soil first. Carelessness where such weeds are concerned might result in the need for a complete overhaul after the end of the first season.

DIGGING

Nowadays, few of us have either the time or the inclination to carry out the digging procedure known as trenching. In this operation, the position of the top and lower spits is reversed, the former going down below and the latter coming up to the surface. In any case, it is doubtful whether this has any advantage over the much easier method of double digging—often referred to as 'bastard trenching'—except perhaps in old gardens, where the topsoil is worn out and infertile.

Digging happens to be one of my favourite garden occupations. There are few pleasanter tasks on a sunny day in winter or spring than the leisurely turning over of the soil and few more conducive to pleasureable meditation.

In digging, the Latin proverb, *Festina lente* (Make haste slowly) is especially applicable. Nothing will be gained, apart from an aching back, by trying to work against the clock where this particular garden task is concerned.

There is an old gardening adage that runs, 'Dig with a spade if you can—with a fork if you must.' This is just another way of saying that the fork is often the better tool for heavy, hard to work soils, while the spade is to be preferred for lighter soils and friable loams that turn over easily.

Ideally, the preparatory digging for a border site should be carried out in autumn or early winter so that frost and drying winds can break down the large clods to the fine tilth needed for planting. For new gardens on heavy clay this is practically essential; those fortunate enough to garden on light sandy loam can dig at almost any time of the year. In any case initial cultivation of the site should be completed at least a month before planting is due to begin in order that the soil has time to settle.

DOUBLE DIGGING

The first operation is to take out a trench one spit (approximately 1ft) deep and 2ft wide, barrowing all the soil away to the other end of the site. The lower spit of soil in this trench is then broken up thoroughly with the fork to the depth of another foot. Any available humus-rich material (well rotted manure or garden compost, leafmould, spent hops or, if you live within carting distance, seaweed) can be mixed well into the lower spit at this stage.

If the site consists of lawn or pasture, the turf can be skimmed off as digging proceeds and can be laid, face downwards, in the trenches before filling in with topsoil from the next strip of digging. This will rot down slowly to provide valuable humus during the first season or two. Annual weeds, such as chickweed or groundsel can also go in on top of this lower spit.

Beware, however, of the perennial weeds such as dock, dandelion, couch grass, creeping buttercup and those two worst scourges of all, bindweed and ground elder. Plots that are badly infested with any of these should be allowed to lie fallow for a season or have early potatoes planted to clean the ground.

Bindweed and ground elder have been the bane of many a garden that I have made. They are most often met with when a neglected garden is taken over or reclaimed—an operation that is often considerably more difficult than starting a new one from stratch. If the smallest fragment of root of either of these weeds is left in the soil, a new plant will result.

Bindweed can be particularly troublesome in a new border. Its spiralling roots burrow to depths of 18in or more, are extremely brittle and practically impossible to get out in their entirety. Docks and dandelions have long probing roots that need to be removed completely if top growth is not to develop afresh.

Sites that are really badly weed infested can be treated with sodium chlorate or a sodium chlorate based weedkiller. After use, the ground will have to lie fallow for six months until all traces of the chemical have been leached out of the soil. Great care must be taken to avoid spread to neighbouring plants or seepage into lawns or grass verges abutting on the border site.

To go back, however, to the double digging. After the first trench has been filled in with the topsoil from the second stretch of digging, the lower spit of the latter gets the same treatment as before. The process is repeated until the far end of the border site is reached. At this stage an experienced or lucky digger will be left with a trench just large enough to accommodate the soil barrowed there at the beginning.

In practice, however, it doesn't always work out like this. Usually he will be left with too much or too little. A bit of raking and levelling, however, will soon put matters right.

SOIL TYPES

The type of soil in the garden will determine, to a certain extent, the kinds of border plants you will be able to grow successfully. It can vary from sticky clay, virtually unworkable except for a few short weeks in autumn and spring, to hot, hungry sand which swallows up manures and fertilisers as fast as they are applied; it can vary, too, from acid peat to alkaline chalk.

Testing the degree of acidity or alkalinity of the soil is a simple matter. Soil-testing kits are available from garden shops and centres, as well as from horticultural chemists. A simple kit is obtainable very cheaply. More sophisticated and expensive kinds which, in addition to the above tests, will determine where chemicals and trace elements necessary to healthy growth are present, are also obtainable.

One or other of these should prove a worthwhile investment. Fortunately, the majority of popular hardy perennials are not unduly fussy where acidity or alkalinity is concerned. A few, however, including lupins, are limehaters while pinks, carnations and perennial scabious require an alkaline soil if they are to be seen at their best. And if calcifuges such as rhododendrons, azaleas and camellias are to form part of a mixed planting of shrubs and perennials, a neutral or acid soil is essential.

The amount of alkalinity or acidity is measured by what is known as the pH factor. Soils with a pH factor of below 7 are acid, those above this figure are alkaline. If your soil should fall in the middle of the scale, at a figure of around 7, you can count yourself extremely lucky. This type of soil can be adapted easily to suit the needs of almost any perennial or shrub.

Excess acidity can be counteracted by applications of lime. This should be applied in the form of hydrated lime or basic slag. Take care, however, since this process can be easily overdone. After a first application, successive ones should be applied with caution and in moderation.

Combating alkalinity is much more difficult, virtually impossible in fact, except over small areas of soil where watering with sequestrene iron will permit lime-hating plants to be grown.

If you have been generous with organic manures when preparing the border site, there should be no need for additional feeding during the first two seasons. Just the same, I prefer to make doubly sure by forking in a top-dressing of bonemeal at the rate of 2oz to the square yard a week or so before planting is due to begin. This slow acting organic fertiliser is rich in phosphorus and a source of nitrogen and calcium. It will, therefore, cater for a large proportion of the plants' needs during the first season.

CHAPTER THREE

Planting the Border

Now the border should be all set for planting-up. Wise gardeners will have placed orders for shrubs and perennials with their nurserymen some months in advance of this date. Alternatively, there is a wide choice of border plants and shrubs available, in ever increasing variety, from garden centres on a cash-and-carry basis.

Buying from garden centres offers the opportunity to see exactly what you are buying and how much plant you are getting for your money. Although container-grown plants can go in at almost any time of the year, they often take longer to get established than plants from the open ground, put in at the proper season.

The first thing is to decide on some kind of planting plan. Whether this is carried in the head or carefully mapped to scale on paper depends largely on the temperament of the planner and on his or her ability to visualise the finished result when there is nothing else but bare earth and a collection of dormant plants.

Unless I were contemplating way-out colour groupings, I should be inclined to dispense with planning on paper and to play the planting—if such an expression can be used horticulturally—by ear. Even with a plan, there are almost certain to be mistakes of overcrowding, under-planting or clashing colours.

Where the perennial plantings are concerned, such mistakes are easily rectified, since they can be transplanted and regrouped at the end of the season. With shrubs, however, it is better to be sure of their positions in the first place. For the benefit of those who like to work from a plan, I have included several, for different kinds of borders, in Chapter 11.

The best time of year to plant the majority of hardy perennials is in October. Planted at this time, they will be established enough to get away to a rapid start the following spring. Where a new border is concerned this is not always practicable. Plants tend to get collected piecemeal, some from nurseries, others from local markets or garden centres and others still—and these can form a valuable nucleus of many new borders—from generous neighbours and gardening friends.

As long as weather conditions are favourable, most perennials can go in at any time from October to March. The major exceptions are grey and silver-leaved subjects and those with woolly or felted leaves such as catmint, artemisias, stachys, verbascums and partly tender perennials such as the brilliant scarlet *Lobelia fulgens,* all of which should be planted in spring.

Never plant when the ground is soggy and waterlogged after heavy rain, or when there is frost in the soil. If planting conditions are unsuitable, plants that arrive from nurserymen can be left in their packing materials for up to a fortnight providing they are not allowed to dry out. If bad weather continues longer than this, the wrappings should be removed and the plants heeled into a trench until they can go into their proper positions. Container-grown plants can stand out in a sheltered part of the garden until you are ready for them.

Where a plan is being used, this can be roughly transferred to the site by marking out positions for the various plant groups with a pointed stick or by outlining them with a dribble of sand or lime. At this stage, it is a good idea to label each section with the name of the plant or plants that are going to occupy it. Any plants available can then be laid out in position, ready to go in.

Wrappings or containers should remain in place until you are actually ready to plant. Drying winds can play havoc with some kinds of plant and losses can occur if the roots are allowed to dry out. Others, like michaelmas daisies, can be left out of the ground all through the winter without coming to any harm.

Planting holes must be roomy and deep enough to accommodate the roots of the plants without bunching or overcrowding. Even when the holes are large and deep enough, it is asking for trouble to stuff new plants into heavy clay soils. In such conditions it is hard for the roots to start into growth again and they cannot be expected to get away to the best of starts.

On heavy soils, therefore, it will pay to remove the soil from the planting holes and replace it with well-matured compost or with a mixture of peat or leafmould and equal parts good loam. An alternative is to keep a supply of sifted topsoil under cover for filling the planting holes. This can be used when the soil is sticky and unworkable after heavy rain.

The roots should sit firmly on the soil at the base of the holes. To make sure no air pockets are left round the roots, the plants should be shaken gently while the holes are being filled. A final firming-in should be given with the knuckles or, in the case of larger perennials, with the heel. In other words—'put the boot in'. Plants with fleshy, thong-like roots, such as gypsophila, oriental poppies and verbascums, must have holes deep enough to accommodate these long taproots.

There are twenty or more popular perennials that should be considered when forming the nucleus of any collection. These are particularly useful for the garden novice since he can plant them with every assurance of a worthwhile display in their first season.

They are noteworthy for their vigour, colourful flowers, ease of cultivation and, in many instances, for their rapid rate of increase. This last quality can be important where the economics of establishing a new border are concerned. With the high cost of plants nowadays, planting groups of up to a dozen perennials, usually necessary to obtain an effective display, can be an expensive project.

It is a great saving to start off with only one or two of each kind. Vigorous growers will form clumps that can be split up into the required number of plants by the end of their first season. This is important where a border of any appreciable size is being planted up.

Most of the more widely grown border subjects share this desirable characteristic. Michaelmas daisies, which need dividing and replanting annually are a typical example. They are one of the mainstays of the autumn border. In September and October, michaelmas daisies ring down the curtain on the border display in a final blaze of exciting colour.

The first of the perennial asters, to give these plants their proper name, actually come into flower in July. These are members of the *amellus* group and include such attractive varieties as *Aster frikartii* 'Wonder of Stafa' whose large light-blue daisy flowers have a central button of golden stamens, 'Mrs Ralph Woods' a delightful pink michaelmas daisy and 'Moerheim Gem', a deep violet form.

To bridge the gap between these and the main display in autumn there are the varieties in the *novae-angliae* group. These flower in August and September and their name is an indication of their transatlantic origins.

They first arrived in this country from New England as long ago as 1710. The group's best known member is 'Harrington's Pink' a tall plant with striking pink flowers. 'Harrington's Pink' has one disadvantage. The flowers tend to close up in the evenings and when cut for the house. For this reason it has suffered a decline in popularity and those who want a good pink michaelmas daisy now plant 'Patricia Ballard', whose fine large flowers do not share this failing.

'Patricia Ballard' is one of the *novi-belgi* group, which contains the majority of those responsible for the main autumn display. Today there are so many new and better varieties that anyone growing the older kinds would be well advised to up-root them, especially when old borders in which they are growing are in process of renovation.

The name of Ballard crops up frequently among these newer introductions. This is a well deserved tribute to the late Ernest Ballard, to whose expertise in breeding michaelmas daisies we owe such a large debt. Such superb plants as 'Ernest Ballard', a large rosy-crimson double, 'Guy Ballard', deep pink, 'Marie Ballard', light blue and 'Sarah Ballard' deep mauve, make fitting memorials to the skill of the man responsible for their introduction.

None of these varieties grows more than 3ft tall. With others of a similar height they make ideal plants for middle positions. 'Crimson Brocade' and 'Winston Churchill' are two of the best of the so called 'red' varieties—their colour would be better described as beetroot crimson. 'Mistress Quickly' is an unusual violet blue, 'Rembrandt' a deep rose pink and 'Tapestry' is a fine double pink with large flowers.

There are also some taller michaelmas daisies that are useful for bringing colour to the back of the autumn border. These include 'Climax' a late-flowering five-footer with single pale blue flowers, 'Lassie' (4ft) a double pink and 'Blandie' (4ft) a semi-double white whose flowers are especially valuable for cutting.

The dwarf kinds of michaelmas daisy make neat hummocks of bright-green foliage that are later completely smothered in bloom and are all 18in or less in height. The leaves remain attractive throughout the summer and when the flowers are fully opened, each plant will resound to the murmur of countless bees, making their last collection of honey before closing down for the winter.

In exposed situations, these dwarfs have the added advantage of needing no staking or ties. They make a tidy and colourful edging, planted in groups of up to a dozen plants.

'Lady in Blue' with lavender flowers, is one of my favourites. Others well worth growing are 'Jenny', violet-purple, 'Pink Lace' and 'Rose Bonnet' both pale pink and 'Queen of Sheba', an unusual lavender-pink variety.

Michaelmas daisies like a sunny position in rich moisture-retaining soil and do best if they are divided and replanted every other year—every year, in fact, if flowers are required for exhibition.

Much of the work involved in tying and staking the plants can be avoided if the main stems of the taller kinds are shortened to about a foot in mid-June. This makes for a bushier, compact plant, capable of supporting itself without staking.

As soon as the flowers have faded, the old stems should be cut right back to ground level. Left until spring the sharp woody stems of these and other similar perennials can present a definite hazard during clearing-up operations.

As michaelmas daisies are to the autumn border, so are lupins and delphiniums to the early summer display. The former flower in June and early July, delphiniums a few weeks later and also over a longer period. Both make their fullest impact before the border display reaches its zenith.

Lupins do best on light well-drained soils that are reasonably lime free. Although you can buy plants of selected strains, lupins are among the easiest perennials to raise from seed. Sowings out of doors in March and April will produce young plants ready to go out into their permanent quarters the following autumn or spring. Many of these seedling plants will, in fact, produce one flower spike, as a sample, during the first season. This make it easy to select the best for planting out in the border.

Delphiniums are almost an essential ingredient where the planting of a new herbaceous border is under consideration. I would not, however, recommend planting those towering giants that draw gasps of admiration at Chelsea and other leading shows. These, I feel, are plants for the specialist exhibitor, too demanding to be able to compete successfully for food and air with the hoipolloi of the border and with flower spikes that are too tall and and fragile to stand up to buffeting by wind without meticulous attention to tying and staking.

My choice would be from among the Belladonna types, none of which exceed 3½ft in height. Unlike the 6ft varieties of *Delphinium elatum*, these need only a minimum of attention. A few twiggy pea sticks, pushed in around the clumps when growth commences, will provide all the support they need. Belladonna delphiniums have a longer flowering period than that of the taller kinds. It will continue from June through August provided that faded flower spikes are removed before they can set seed. 'Pink Sensation', with flowers of a clear cyclamen-pink, is one of the loveliest of these medium-height delphiniums. Others worth growing are the gentian-blue 'Wendy', 'Lamartine', a deep violet-blue and 'Blue Bees', a free-flowering pale blue variety.

More than most other border plants, delphiniums need a really rich, well cultivated soil. It pays, therefore to spend extra time on the preparation of their planting positions, adding generous supplies of humus-rich material in the shape of rotted animal manure or garden compost and finishing with three or four handfuls of bonemeal in each planting hole.

The young shoots of delphiniums are particularly susceptible to damage by slugs, both above and below soil level. Some kind of preventative, such as Meta fuel mixed with bran, slug pellets or a liquid slug killer should be applied at regular intervals during winter and early spring. A pile of coarse ashes spread over the crown of the plants while they are dormant will also help deter these pests.

Page 35 (above) *Phlox* 'Norah Leigh' grown for its strikingly variegated foliage; (right) *Achillea* 'Moonshine'

Page 36 (above) *Coreopsis verticillata*; (left) *Penstemon barbatus*

IRISES

Another popular race of hardy plants that provide valuable material for the border is the bearded or flag irises, *Iris germanica*. The flowers, on their erect stems, provide a magnificent early summer display. By a careful choice of varieties, their flowering season can be extended from late April to mid-July. Their sword like leaves, too, make an interesting contrast to the rounded shapes of other neighbouring perennials.

The iris is one of the oldest of our cultivated plants. It was grown in Egypt when the boy king, Tutankhamun, was sitting on his throne. Its flower is the origin of the *fleur-de-lis* with its princely and scouting associations. Today, the iris, as well as being a favourite garden plant has become a specialists' flower, with a national society in Britain as well as a separate group within the Royal Horticultural Society.

The varieties on offer today are a far cry from and an incredible improvement on the old purple flags. Colours range from purest white through pinks, lavenders and purples to a deep velvety violet that would almost pass for black.

The rhizomatous irises are the kind most widely grown. These, more than any others, have been the major preoccupation of the specialist growers and breeders. The 'fans' of swordlike leaves spring from a perennial fleshy rhizome. When they are planted, this should rest on the soil surface, to absorb sunshine. It will be firmly anchored by strong fibrous roots.

The bearded iris likes a place in full sun and a well drained alkaline soil. When the rhizomes are planted, their upper surface should be clear of the soil for the reasons already mentioned.

The best time for planting, as well as for dividing and replanting, is as soon as the plants have finished flowering. Nurserymen, therefore, normally send out plants in July or August. When you plant, as long as the border soil is in good

c

heart, a few handfuls of bonemeal should be enough to get the young plants away to a good start before winter.

Do not expect a startling display from bearded irises in their first season after planting. One flower spike is good growth from each plant but once the clumps are established, flowering will become prolific. After the third or fourth season, the clumps will probably need dividing and transplanting. When this is done, the worn out rhizomes at the centre should be discarded. Only the younger and plumper ones from the outside should be replanted. The leaves can be shortened by two-thirds before planting. This will reduce their wind resistance and give the anchoring roots a better chance of becoming established.

In badly drained soils, iris rhizomes are sometimes attacked by a fungus disease known as rhizome rot. Planting too deeply makes them more susceptible. Plants that are affected should be dug up and have the affected parts of the rhizomes cut away and dusted with flowers of sulphur before replanting.

VARIETIES

'White City' is one of the best white irises, noteworthy for its absolute purity of colour. Pink, a relatively new colour break in irises, is represented by such delightful varieties as 'Party Dress', 'Powder Pink' and the paler 'Pink Cameo'. 'Top Flight' has flowers that are a blend of amber and apricot, set off by an orange beard.

Among the many lovely blues my choice for the border would be that old favourite, 'Aline', with others equally popular, such as 'Arabi Pasha', an intense corn-flower blue and 'Jane Phillips' with attractively ruffled flax-blue petals. 'Enchanted Violet' is a pale mauve iris with touches of pink in the falls and outer petal. It has an orange beard.

Other proven varieties include the blue-black 'Black Hills' and 'Black Ink', 'Mabel Chadburn', one of the finest yellows,

'Ola Kala' a brilliant orange-yellow iris with flared and ruffled petals and 'Prairie Sunset', whose flowers are a medley of pink, apricot-gold and coppery-bronze.

All the varieties mentioned above are reasonable in price and easy to grow. Getting bitten by the iris bug can, however, be a costly business; and this is particularly true when one is buying plants of new varieties. Any of those I have mentioned should be obtainable quite inexpensively at the time of writing. This list of good varieties could be extended to include others such as the mulberry-purple 'Master Charles' and 'Benton Evora', a distinctive orchid purple. There are some others, equally worthwhile, ranging in colour from rosy red to deepest crimson—varieties that include 'Indian Chief', 'Right Royal' and 'Solid Mahogany'.

Choose, for the bearded irises, a position in full sun near to or at the front of the border. They average 2½-3ft in height although some, like the stately 'White City' have flower spikes 4ft tall.

The Siberian irises, which also flower in June, make useful and trouble-free border plants, with dainty flowers, rather like those of the bulbous irises, poised, like iridescent butterflies on slender stems. Each plant has a profusion of bloom although their flowering season is all too brief. But the clumps of rush-like foliage provide continuing interest and are good weed suppressors.

Iris sibirica varieties are obtainable in a fairly wide range of colours, including 'Snow Queen', white with a yellow marking on the falls; 'Papillon'; 'Cambridge Blue'; 'Perry's Blue', sky-blue; 'Helen Astor', lilac-pink; 'Caesar', and 'Emperor', both violet-blue and 'Eric the Red', wine-red. These range in height from 2½ to 4ft.

PHLOX

Phlox have such a high popularity rating among hardy perennials that they, too, must qualify for inclusion in the basic planting of a border. They possess two outstanding qualities —brilliance and wide range of colour and an incredibly long flowering season, lasting from early July well into September.

In general, border phloxes are hybrid forms of *Phlox paniculata*. The type plant had a mauve flower. This colouring continued practically unchanged until well into the present century. Then, under the expert care of the late Captain Symons-Jeune and others, a whole new breed of phloxes emerged with much larger and more colourful flower trusses and individual florets.

Phlox need a rich, well cultivated and well drained soil. They should not be allowed to dry out during summer. To prevent this, the soil in and around their planting positions should be enriched with the addition of plenty of humus in the shape of well rotted manure or garden compost, leafmould, peat or spent hops.

Mention of this last material may prompt the question as to its availability. Unlike the proprietary hop manures which have hops as a basis, but rely mainly on their beneficial effect on the incorporation of inorganic fertilisers such as sulphate of ammonia and sulphate of potash, spent hops are just what their name implies, the residue of normal brewing processes. They are obtainable from your local brewery on a cash-and-carry basis. At one time, you could take away as much as your available transport could carry for well under a pound.

Today, spent hops are less easy to obtain. Many breweries dispose of their surpluses to the fertiliser manufacturers. Seaweed which is rich in essential plant nutrients and trace elements, is an excellent substitute for any of the materials mentioned.

Phlox colours range from pure white through pink, salmon, scarlet and crimson to rich purple. So far there is no true blue although a number of varieties have colours that almost approximate to it including the violet-blue 'Russian

Violet', lavender-blue 'Skylight' and periwinkle blue 'Bleu de Pervenche'. Heights range, according to variety from 18in in the dwarf white 'Mia Ruys' up to 4ft in the soft pink 'Rosa Spier'. This means that there are kinds suitable for any position in the border.

Self colours are the most popular but many varieties have flowers with an 'eye' of contrasting colour, rather like those of the old auricula-eyed sweet williams. 'Rosa Spier', mentioned above, is one of these, with a deep crimson eye that contrasts well with the surrounding pink. Others with this characteristic are 'Olive', salmon pink, and 'Firefly', a paler pink. Both have a contrasting crimson eye. Among the finest self colours are 'Brigadier', a striking salmon-orange phlox, 'Lilac Time', pale lilac, 'Mother of Pearl', the palest of pinks, 'San Antonio', deep wine-red and 'White Admiral', a fine pure white.

A variety called 'Nora Leigh' is enjoying great popularity at present. This is a maverick among phloxes. Nora Leigh is grown primarily for the decorative effect of its green-and-gold variegated foliage. The small mauve flowers are insignificant.

Wherever space permits, phlox look their best planted in large drifts of up to a dozen. This enables their colour, as well as their spicy fragrance, to be enjoyed to the full.

PEONIES

Herbaceous peonies are among the loveliest of all the hardy border perennials and some of the most rewarding to grow. A peony plant represents a valuable long-term garden investment. Left undisturbed, it will declare a lifetime of dividends of unsurpassed beauty. Peonies were described by the ancient Greeks as the oldest of plants. They were certainly being cultivated in China and Japan many centuries before the birth of Christ. One of their most surprising qualities is their longevity. There are records of plants that have flowered and flourished in the same position for fifty years or more. They greatly resent being disturbed, however, and plants should be lifted only when it is absolutely necessary.

Peonies like a deep, rich and well drained soil, generously supplied with humus. They appreciate a yearly winter top dressing of well-rotted manure or compost. Given this, they do not object to a certain amount of shade and can be grown in the dappled shadow of fruit trees or the less dense ornamental trees such as silver birch, Japanese cherries or flowering crabs. They do not succeed under the denser shade of woodland trees or conifers.

Peonies have long thonglike taproots that are usually shortened before they leave the nursery. They must not be planted too deeply since this will inhibit their full flowering potential. The crimson growth buds, which are easily discernible on the rootstock when the plants are dormant, should never be more than 2in below soil level.

Peonies normally take a few seasons to come into their full flower production. Once this stage is reached, they throw up more and more flowering stems each spring. Since they will not be moved, plenty of room must be left between the plants for subsequent spread—up to 4ft for the more vigorous kinds.

The earliest to come into flower, starting in the second or third week in May, are varieties of the old cottage peony. They open their petal-packed blooms in the second or third week in May. *Paeonia officinalis* has large globular flowers rather like those of the old fashioned cabbage roses. The two best known varieties are *P.o. rosea plena* and *P.o. rubra,* pink and crimson respectively. There is also a fine double white form, *P.o. alba plena.* 'Sunshine' is a brilliant scarlet and there is a garnet-red single, 'J. C. Weguelin', with a striking central boss of golden anthers.

When we come to the June-flowering *P. lactiflora* (syn *P. albiflora*) the choice of varieties is so wide as to be almost embarrassing. They run into hundreds. On looking through

specialist catalogues one cannot fail to notice the constant
repetition of the name Kelway among these. This is not surprising since the Kelways of Langport have played an all important role in the development of this outstanding race of
plants. Any to which their name has been given are particularly worth growing.

'Kelway's Glorious' is considered by many to be the finest of
all the double white forms. Pinks, too, are well represented by
such varieties as 'Kelway's Lovely', whose rosy petals are
suffused with creamy pink. 'Kelway's Supreme', like 'Kelway's
Glorious', is another top ranking variety with very large
blush-pink blooms that turn almost white when fully open.
This particular peony has a longer flowering season than
most others which makes it a good choice where one or only
a few varieties are grown. 'James Kelway', another white,
whose flowers are faintly tinged with pink, is another long-
flowering kind. Both these two last named are in bloom continuously from late May right through to July. Other worthwhile varieties are 'Albert Crousse', shell-pink, 'Duchesse de
Nemours', white with a hint of pale yellow, 'Marie Crousse',
coral-pink turning white and 'Shimmering Velvet', a volup-
tuous-looking dark crimson.

These are all doubles. The singles, however, have their own
particular charm since the petals unfold to display a striking
crown of golden anthers. Whitleyi major, also named, more
aptly, 'The Bride', is one of the finest of these with large pure-
white blooms on tall stems. 'Lord Kitchener' is a deep-maroon
single, 'Queen Elizabeth' has flowers of a pale flesh pink.
Practically all varieties of *P. lactiflora* have a delicious
fragrance.

No collection of herbaceous peonies would be complete
without some of the newer 'Imperial' types. These differ
from the conventional singles in having a mass of petaloids
(petals that have undergone a botanical change and become
narrowed and attractively twisted) at the centre of each cup-

shaped bloom. The petalioids are often in a constrasting colour to the outer ring of petals proper. 'Bowl of Beauty', pale pink and 'Gleam of Light' carmine-pink with cream and yellow petaloids are two of the most noteworthy of these.

TREE PEONIES

Equally valuable for the herbaceous border are the somewhat ineptly-named tree peonies or Moutans. These are mainly varieties and hybrid forms of *P. suffruticosa*. Far from being treelike in habit, they are deciduous shrubby plants which seldom exceed 5ft at maturity. They flower from early May up to the middle of June. Their compact habit makes them ideal shrubs to associate with perennials in the border.

Like the herbaceous forms, the tree peony is one of the oldest known plants on record. Mention of them appears in Oriental writings as far back as the seventh century. The tree peony was known in ancient China as 'The King of Flowers', a title which it richly deserves.

Tree peonies are distinguished by the striking beauty of their flowers which are similar to, but very much larger than those of the herbaceous kinds. In some varieties they measure as much as 1ft across. The plants flower at an early age and increase in floriferousness in a kind of geometrical progression until one relatively small specimen can produce 100 or more of these lovely blooms.

They will thrive in any good garden soils and have no objection to alkaline conditions. This makes them a useful alternative to the May-flowering azaleas for gardens on chalk or where lime is present in quantity. The plants are normally supplied grafted on to the rootstock of the herbaceous kinds. This means that, unlike the latter, they must be planted deeply with the union between graft and scion well below soil level in order to get away on their own roots. Provided the soil is in good heart, an annual top dressing of bonemeal should satisfy their nutritional requirements.

Tree peonies are extremely hardy and are tolerant of sub-zero temperatures in the region of -40° F. They have, however, a habit of producing new young shoots and flower buds very early in the season. In exposed situations, in colder districts, these are susceptible to frost damage. On cold nights in spring, when night frosts are forecast, it is advisable to protect the plants. Polythene or large sheets of newspaper afford sufficient protection and, since frosty nights are normally still nights, the covering will remain in position by itself. It can be removed the following morning as soon as the frost has thawed.

Their flowering period is relatively short although not more so than that of the azaleas for which they form such a valuable substitute. But both these and the herbaceous kinds provide continuing attraction with their handsome, finely cut foliage. This is a vivid crimson when it first unfurls, colouring again late in the year to bring interest to the autumn border. This makes peonies one of the finest all-rounders.

After the basic plantings have been decided on, it is time to consider the second line of defence. There are any number of worthwhile and popular perennials that can be used for this purpose. Although they may not be available in such a wide variety as those of the plant groups just described, they are all just as indispensable for producing continuity of interest from early spring to late autumn.

BERGENIAS

Among the first to flower, in March and early April are the bergenias, popularly known as giant saxifrages and to the countryman as Pigsqueak or Elephants' Ears. These are evergreen and as useful for their handsome dark-green leathery leaves as for the early arrival of their large and striking flower trusses.

The bergenias have a host of garden virtues. They flourish in the driest conditions as well as in dense shade. This makes them ideal subjects for the shadier parts of a border or for positions under any trees or shrubs that may be included in the border planting plan. Once established, they provide excellent ground cover, smothering even the most persistent weeds under their carpet of heavy foliage.

There are several distinct species and hybrids, the best known of which is *Bergenia cordifolia*. This has bronzy, spoon-shaped foliage and pale pink flowers. There is a variety, *purpurea,* with flowers of a deeper rose crimson than those of the type. *B. crassifolia* has larger, more rounded leaves that turn a brilliant coppery crimson in autumn to provide continuing colour until the paler young leaves unfurl in spring.

B. delavayii is another fine species, also noteworthy for its winter leaf colouring. There are, as well, several outstanding named varieties and hybrids, including 'Evening Glow' with dark purple-red flowers, 'Silver Light', an unusual white bergenia whose florets have pink calyces and perhaps the most striking of them all, 'Ballawley Hybrid', also listed as 'Delbees'. This has the handsomest foliage and the largest flower trusses.

SOME OTHER CURTAIN RAISERS

Another race of early flowering perennials that act as curtain-raisers to the main display, when their yellow daisy flowers appear in April, are the doronicums or leopardsbanes. These form neat, easily manageable clumps with an abundance of flowers. There are several species and varieties but the one most commonly seen is *Doronicum plantagineum* 'Harpur Crewe'. This bears its flowers erect on tall stems and is a real asset to the early spring border.

'Spring Beauty' is a newer cultivar with deeper yellow double blooms. It flowers later than the former. Lesser known kinds include *D. austriacum,* whose golden-yellow flowers appear 2-3 to a stem and *D. caucasicum,* a dwarf species with small golden flowers.

In spite of its name, the Pasque flower, *Pulsatilla vulgaris,* seldom manages to live up to this unless Easter falls very late, although plants in sheltered positions usually manage to produce their unusual purple flowers during the first or second week of April. Unusual because the flowers, as well as the leaves and stems of this delightful little plant, are covered with a silvery silken down. The rounded silky seedheads which follow the flowers are almost as decorative. Pulsatillas should be planted young since they resent disturbance.

Another perennial that flowers early is that old favourite of the cottage garden, *Dicentra spectabilis.* This is a lovely plant on several counts. The soft ferny foliage is always attractive and provides a perfect setting for the arching sprays of pink-and-white pendent lyre-shaped flowers that appear in May and early June.

Dicentra spectabilis is a plant of many aliases. In addition to the name by which it is known best, Bleeding Heart, it also answers, in various parts of the country, to Lyre Flower, Lady's Locket, Dutchman's Breeches and Our Lady in a Boat. All these names are inspired by the colouring and unusual form of the flowers.

Pulmonarias, or lungworts, are also first class plants for providing pools of colour in the border early in the year. The genus includes several kinds with attractively spotted leaves, the best of which is *P. saccharata,* variously known as Spotted Dog or Soldiers and Sailors. The creamy spots on its leaves are responsible for the first name, the second is on account of its flowers which open reddish-brown and turn blue.

There is a newer variety known as 'Pink Dawn', with rose-pink flowers. 'Munstead Blue', a fine form of the closely-related but narrower-leaved *P. angustifolia* has flowers of an intense gentian-blue. *P. angustifolia* is a valuable ground-cover plant, spreading rapidly in a few seasons to form a close weed-smothering carpet.

June will see the border display really getting under way, with many well-known perennials such as Oriental poppies, pyrethrums, lupins, anchusa, aquilegias, geums and many others making their colour contribution. But it is in July and August that it reaches its peak with phlox, penstemons, Shasta daisies, delphiniums, heleniums, rudbeckias and a host of well-known and lesser-known subjects that are described in detail in Chapter 7.

CHAPTER FOUR

Lesser-Known Perennials

Most of the plants already mentioned are practically indispensable to any border planting. But for in-filling between the groups of border favourites, personal preferences can be indulged more freely.

For the newcomer to gardening, one of the best ways of finding out about these more out of the ordinary subjects is to see them actually growing in their proper surroundings. Catalogue descriptions are a useful guide but they cannot be a substitute for a look at the actual plants *in situ*. Visits to nurseries and garden centres may give some sort of idea but any plants seen will be mainly immature. Prospective buyers will have only a sketchy idea of the ultimate height, spread and form. Other sources of information and interest will be found in public gardens and parks and no one within travelling distance should fail to visit the Royal Horticultural Society's gardens at Wisley in Surrey, where there are fine examples of island and mixed borders.

In any of these borders worthy of note you will find that, in addition to relying on colour, great emphasis is placed on beauty of form and foliage. Many of the lesser-known perennials possess these qualities and some, at least ought to be included when preliminary planning is under consideration.

One of my own favourites in this case is the oddly named Bears' Breeches or acanthus. I grow these primarily for the beauty of their handsome sculptured foliage which, as garden writers never tire of informing us, served as a model for the carved Corinthian capitals of ancient Greek temples and monuments.

The two species commonly seen in gardens are *Acanthus mollis* and *A. spinosus*. They are easily distinguishable by their leaves, prickly and thistle-like in *spinosus* and with smoother, fluted margins in *mollis*. Both species have bold 4ft spires of hooded flowers. Those of *A. mollis* are white and lilac pink; *A. spinosus* has white and purple flowers with showy jade-green bracts. In normal garden conditions the leaves of both species are evergreen.

The acanthuses like a sunny, well drained situation and although severe frost may cause damage to their top growth, the plants themselves are completely hardy. Fresh stocks are easily obtained from seed or by propagation from root cuttings.

Most gardeners are familiar with the prickly sea hollies, with their steely teazle-like flowers and bracts. Most of them are perennials but there is one biennial species worthy of inclusion. *Eryngium giganteum* has sea-green flower heads that turn a silvery white as they mature. This species is sometimes known as 'Miss Willmott's Ghost'. That great plantswoman of the early years of this century, Ellen Willmott, was reputed to have scattered a few seeds of this plant when visiting other gardens, to the subsequent surprise of their owners when these offbeat plants appeared.

My own preference is for the American eryngiums. These were comparatively rare until recently but I see from my catalogues that they are now more readily obtainable. They are evergreen and in winter their decorative rosettes of toothed leaves might easily be mistaken for those of one of the smaller yuccas or aloes.

E. agavifolium, as its Latin name implies, is one of those that are aloelike in character, sprouting, from its basal rosette of leaves, 3ft branching spikes of cone flowers. *E. bromelii-*

folium has narrower, more deeply toothed leaves with 5ft flower stems massed candelabra fashion with small white flowers something like those of partly opened pussy-willow. Both species flower in July.

All the eryngiums like a position in full sun and although reputed to dislike disturbance, I have never had any difficulty either in dividing established clumps or in replanting in a new position. This may be because the plants are out of the ground only for the time that it takes to transfer them from one place to another in the garden. I have found that many reputedly difficult movers can be shifted successfully providing they are lifted with a good ball of soil round their roots and are put into their new position with a minimum of delay.

Although most gardeners grow one species of hellebore, the Christmas rose, *Helleborus niger,* that is not normally the kind of perennial one would expect to find in the average herbaceous border since it does best growing among shrubs in conditions of partial shade. This is partly true, as well, of other hellebore species but most of them are so decorative, not only when actually in flower but also during the incredibly long period that the lime-green seed heads continue to provide interest, that they are deserving of a place in any shady moist spot available.

H. corsicus is the tallest and most eye catching of the hellebore species, with large heads of apple-green cups lasting from early spring well into summer. The magnificent toothed foliage is evergreen as is also that of our unkindly named native species, the stinking hellebore, *H. foetidus.* The flower heads of the latter are not as large as those of *corsicus* but compensate for this by the beauty of their purple-margined petals. The leaves of *H. foetidus* are finely divided into narrow, saw-toothed segments. It comes into flower some weeks earlier than *H. corsicus.*

There is a superb hybrid form of this last-named species, *H.* x *sternii* (*H. corsicus* x *H. lividus*) in which the leaves are

distinctively marbled and the flowers have an attractive
purple tinge.

It is among the Lenten roses (*H. orientalis* and its many
hybrids) that the most striking developments have occurred.
These flower from November to March and the older strains
had a colour range from creamy white through varying shades
of pink to purple. Nowadays, it is possible to get strains in
which one colour predominates such as the Constellation
strain whose pink flowers are tinged with green and speckled
with maroon; Pink Strain, with flowers that range from a delicate shell-pink to soft rose and Midnight Sky strain, whose
flowers are a royal purple spotted with an even deeper colour.

For many years the legendary slate-grey hellebore, *H. tor-
quata* appeared to have shared the fate of the scented musk
and disappeared completely from cultivation. Now, however,
it has been rediscovered and a new hybrid clone, bred by Eric
Smith has been introduced to garden commerce. This has
similar slate-blue flowers but a more open and branching
habit. The name of this new hybrid is 'Pluto'.

Hellebores like a rich soil and do well on limy soils. A
mulch of well rotted compost in spring and a dressing of
bonemeal in autumn will keep the plants in good condition.
Most hellebore species violently resent disturbance although
on occasion I have moved quite large and established clumps
of *H. orientalis* without any apparent harm.

The hostas, or plantain lilies are primarily grown for the
beauty of their foliage and begin to display this as the hellebores are going over. Hostas are among the handsomest foliage
plants for a herbaceous border, with their magnificent ribbed
plantain-like leaves, in some species 2ft or more in length and
half as much across. The plants develop, fairly slowly, into
extensive clumps of weed smothering foliage, perfect for any
setting, whether in sun or shade.

Although hostas, like hellebores, do best in partial shade,
they will be quite happy in full sun provided they are given

Page 53 *Crinum powelli* one of the most striking bulbous subjects for association with perennials

Page 54   Polyanthus of contrasting colours used to edge a border

plenty of water during dry periods in summer. In sunny positions, the tall spires of lily-like blooms, which I regard solely as a pleasant bonus, will be more numerous and less drawn up. In most hosta species, these are pale lilac or mauve, although *Hosta elata* and *H. sieboldiana* both have white flowers.

The species with the boldest and largest leaves is *H. sieboldiana* (syn *H. glauca*). The plants can vary a good deal in their leaf colouring. Some forms have much bluer foliage than that of the type. The leaf veins are deeply etched. There is also a variety 'Elegans' with deeply corrugated and crinkled leaves and one with pure white flowers, 'Alba'.

The species with variegated leaves are valuable in the border for the contrast that they provide to the more predominant green of perennial foliage. They are also useful as a barrier between two areas of clashing colour. *H. albo-marginata* is one of the best of these with grey-green leaves narrowly margined with white. One of the most striking, when its leaves first appear in spring, is *H. fortunei* 'Albo-Picta'. This has bright golden leaves with a darker green edge which slowly turn to a more uniform green as the season progresses. The variety 'Aureo-marginata' has similar leaf colouring but in reverse, with gold rimming the edges of its foliage. Both these forms grow between $1\frac{1}{2}$ and 2ft tall.

'Thomas Hogg' is one of the finest named cultivars. The deep green leaves have a wide margin of white. *H. crispula*, too, is particularly worthy of note. Although the leaf markings are similar to that of the former, the foliage has the added interest of crimped and fluted edges.

Day-lilies, or hemerocallis, are among the best of the dual-purpose perennials for a long display. In addition to their colourful trumpet flowers they have attractive rushlike foliage that makes effective ground cover. Day-lilies are very easy to grow and favour any kind of soil, wet or dry, heavy or light. Their apple-green leaves are among the first to break

D

surface in spring. The flowers, on tall stout stems, appear
from May to July according to variety. They continue to
flower over a very long period. The name day-lily is an accur-
ate description as far as the individual flowers on each spike
are concerned since these normally open and fade in a single
day. There are, however, always any number of buds waiting
to take over and since the flowers on each spike come out two
or three at a time, the spikes are always attractive in appearance.

Day-lilies have undergone a striking transformation in the
past decade or so. Countless new varieties and hybrids have
made their bow, a tremendous improvement on the older
orange and yellow forms. This is due to the attention of the
specialist breeders. They have not only extended the colour
range and beauty of form of the flowers, but also their flowering season so that some kinds can now be had in bloom as
early as May.

Colours now range from pale lemon, through apricot and
orange to dark crimsons verging on black. 'Pink Damask',
being the nearest approach to a pure pink day-lily to date, is
particularly lovely. Among the best yellows are 'Bonanza',
'Burford', 'Golden West' and 'Primrose Mascotte'. Of the
stronger orange and crimson colours, 'Orangeman' (apricot-
orange), 'Apollo' (similar but with crimson-edged petals)
'Helios' (coppery red), 'Old Vintage' (deep copper red with a
pale yellow throat) and 'Black Prince' (blackish crimson with
a lemon throat) are all well worth growing.

Day-lilies are easily increased by division of the clumps in
spring.

Although the euphorbias, or spurges, whose attraction lies
largely in their handsome bracts, greenish yellow or lime
green in most species, are not plants to everyone's taste, I
would not like to be without at least a few in the garden.
Apart from the interest they bring to the border from spring
to midsummer, they are in great demand by the flower

arrangers. For someone like myself, whose wife is profession-
ally involved in this occupation, growing them is virtually
a 'must'. They are one of my favourite plant families and one
which, together with hostas and hellebores are well worth the
attention of anyone who fancies himself as a plant collector.
Some, like *Euphorbia wulfenii* and *E. characias* are classed as
shrubs but their habit is so like that of an evergreen perennial that they associate perfectly with herbaceous plants.

Among my favourites is *E. epithymoides* (syn *E. poly-
chroma*). This gives broad hints of the beauty to come in
March or early April when the partly opened buds display a
vivid citron yellow. In the space of a few weeks the plants are
smothered in a mass of lime-green flowers, whose attraction
lasts for many weeks as they gradually fade to a paler green.
E. epithymoides is as neat a border plant as anyone could
wish for. It forms a rounded clump that gives a neat appearance to the edge of the border. I plant in groups of six or
more and divide the plants every third season. Stocks are
easily increased in this way.

There is a slightly taller species, *E. pilosa major,* with
similar flowers to those of *E. epithymoides*. This is useful
where a drift of plants has to be continued towards the middle
of the border. It grows 1½ to 2ft tall as against the 1ft of *E.
epithymoides*. It also declares an attractive autumn bonus in
the shape of pink-tinged foliage that later turns bright gold.

Another attractive low-growing spurge is *E. myrsinites,* a
prostrate type with scaly blue-grey leaves, close packed on
their stems, snaking out from a single crown. This is an ideal
plant for a sunny bank or dry wall, but it can also be used to
advantage as an edging plant where a border abuts on to a
paved walk, where it will help to soften the hard lines of the
edge. *E. myrsinites* is especially lovely in late spring when
each of the previous year's trailing shoots is tipped with clusters of lime-green, reddish-centred bracts.

Another attractive early-flowering spurge is *E. robbiae,*

with dark-green leathery leaves rather like those of small rhododendron. The flowers, in loose cylindrical clusters are borne on 18in stems. This species has a particularly rapid rate of spread which makes it an excellent cover-and-smother plant. In small gardens, however, its invasive habits will need keeping in check. This warning also applies to *E. sikkimensis* which flowers later—towards midsummer—and has paler leaves veined with coppery red. Together with *E. robbiae,* it is one of the best species for a wild or woodland border, since both do well in shady conditions.

Most people are surprised to find that the scarlet poinsettias, so much in demand as winter house plants, are actually members of the spurge family and are botanically known as *Euphorbia pulcherrima.* Poinsettias are not hardy out of doors in Britain, although they grow like the proverbial weeds in Mediterranean countries. I have vivid memories of picking enormous bunches in Egypt on Christmas day as decorations for the festive table.

Although the completely hardy *E. griffithii* cannot compare with this exotic relation for brilliance of impact, its smaller flame-coloured bracts still make a considerable splash of colour when they appear in early summer. There are also several spurges native to the British Isles, including the biennial caper spurge, *E. lathyris* which is reputed to drive away moles. This reputation, in my garden at any rate is totally undeserved, since moles practically gambol at the foot of a group of plants put in specifically with this purpose in mind.

The only native species worth a place in the border is *E. palustris,* a giant of a plant with large heads of yellow bracts on 4ft stems in April.

Finally, there are two truly magnificent shrubby species of spurge, *E. wulfenii* and the lesser known but equally attractive *E. characias.* The former grows about 4ft tall (there is also a variety *sibthorpii* that tops 6ft) and both have dark evergreen foliage and large flue-brush spikes of lime-green flowers. *E. characias* is distinguished by the coppery red eye at the centre of each individual floret.

CHAPTER FIVE

Maintenance of the Border

In the years between the wars, the herbaceous border, for so long a predominant feature of gardens both large and small, suffered a decline in popularity. In larger gardens, this was due to difficulties in finding suitable labour and the increased costs of garden upkeep. Only tycoons could afford to employ large staffs of gardeners and one of the first features to be scrapped was usually the herbaceous border, with its time and labour-consuming tasks of planting, weeding, staking, tying, dividing and replanting.

Smaller gardens, too, felt the crunch as weekend distractions like sport and motoring came within the reach of almost everyone. The decline caused by these and other similar factors was accelerated during World War II. Many famous borders were dug up 'for victory' and potatoes took the place of peonies. From being difficult, labour problems now became virtually impossible, with only green-fingered ladies of more than a certain age left behind to carry on the traditions of the pleasure garden.

This, one might imagine, should have sounded the death knell of the herbaceous border completely by dealing this kind of gardening a blow from which it could not recover. Surprisingly, however, this was not the case. Given a face-lift and with radical changes in its makeup, the herbaceous border is as popular a garden feature today as it ever was.

For this, we can thank a number of different factors, most of them directed towards the saving of labour. First, and most important, is the use of new kinds of plants and new varieties of old favourites that are sturdy enough to stand up for themselves without the need for tying and staking or with only a minimum of support. New and more compact varieties of such popular plants as goldenrod and michaelmas daisies, for example, have superseded the older and taller kinds that used to keel over into a sprawling mass in the first summer gale. Greater use is being made as well of more permanent plantings, such as peonies, day-lilies and other perennials that need transplanting and dividing infrequently or not at all.

Another important labour-saving innovation lies in the use of ground cover plants to act as weed smotherers while still providing colour and interest. Such plants, decorative in themselves, form dense mats of ground hugging foliage through which only the most persistent weeds are able to penetrate.

Finally there are the newer weedkillers. Some of these can be applied to weeds growing among the plants without harm to the latter, since they are neutralised on contact with the soil. Others have a selective effect, discriminating against emergent annual weeds but harmless to other plants. This type of weedkiller will effectively keep a border free of annual weeds for six weeks or more after each application.

In spite of all this, it would be foolish to imagine that any garden worthy of the name can be made without its full quota of hard work. Maintaining a perennial or mixed border in the style to which it is accustomed is no exception. It should not, however, entail any greater effort or take up more time than looking after annual or bedding plants. Annuals need as much, if not more attention than perennials while bedding schemes need a complete change twice a year.

STAKING

One of the major tasks, where a herbaceous border is concerned, is the provision of support for those plants that need it although, as mentioned above, many of these sprawlers can now be dispensed with. In any case, such support need not necessarily involve complicated tying and staking except in the case of tall floppy subjects such as delphiniums and Oriental poppies or where such plants as dahlias are used to provide continuity of colour in autumn.

For such strong growers as the last named, ordinary stakes or light bamboo canes are of little use. What will be needed is either the special green-painted dahlia stakes or stout bamboos. These should provide sufficient support even in the fiercest of gales.

Staking should begin soon after the plants start into growth. Each stem should be separately secured to a central stake with a loop of garden twine. Bunching all the stems together with one tie is a practice to be avoided. This gives a completely unnatural look, not only to the plants thus treated but also to the overall appearance of the border. Where clumps in need of tying are large, it is better to use several stakes, tying in a few stems to each.

The ties should be repeated at 1ft intervals as growth progresses. For any but the tallest perennials two such ties should be enough. The majority of border plants, however, will need no tying. They can be supported with twiggy peasticks placed in or around the clumps. This will be sufficient for the 'in-betweens'—those plants needing only a minimum of support —while a number of others will need no help at all.

The secret of success with this last method of staking is to get the peasticks into position when the new season's growth is only a few inches tall. Then, as the plants grow on, the sticks provide ample support while the foliage, by the time the flowering stage is reached, will camouflage the support completely to give a completely natural look to the border.

Experienced gardeners soon get to know the vital statistics of their plants. The newcomer to gardening will find the details in Chapter 7, where lists of border plants are given. Remember, however, that any kind of support should finish below the ultimate height of the plant, so nothing will be visible when the border display is at its peak.

WEEDING

In the early years of a border's life, weeding is usually one of the major chores, especially on sites that were formerly rough ground or pasture. As thorough as the initial preparation may be, it is virtually impossible to get rid of all weeds at this stage. Some, like bindweed, have long twisting roots that penetrate several feet below soil level. These make new shoots from every joint so that even the smallest scrap left in the soil is capable of forming a new plant. Cultivation, too, will bring to the surface hosts of dormant annual weed seeds. The resulting seedlings will have to be dealt with before they start to compete for food and air with the rightful occupants of the border.

Two of the methods already mentioned will solve many of these weed problems. Fallowing the site for a season, or putting it down to potatoes, will enable most perennial weeds to be eradicated; treating it with sodium chlorate and leaving it unoccupied for six months or more will do the job even more thoroughly.

Most of us, however, when we take over a new garden or plan new features of an existing one are impatient for results. I, for one, have never allowed the daunting prospect of an entire season spent in battle against docks, dandelions, buttercups and creeping thistles to prevent me from making an immediate start on a new border. In any case, the plants are likely to be fairly thin on the ground during the first season so that it is a fairly easy, albeit a backaching job, to get in among them with the hoe or better still with a handfork, at frequent intervals during the first summer after planting.

Really persistent weeds such as bindweed or ground elder can usually be dealt with satisfactorily by painting the leaves with an extra-strong solution of a hormone weed-killer. Choose a calm day for this operation and take care that none of the liquid is allowed to splash on to leaves of the border plants. Two or three such applications should be enough to put paid to even the worst infestation.

Broad-leaved weeds such as plantains, docks and dandelions can be dealt with by a similar method. An easier way is to use a, paraquat-based weedkiller such as Weedol, which is neutralised on coming into contact with the soil but which is death to both annual and perennial weeds. If annual weeds alone are troublesome, they can be dealt with by applications of a weedkiller such as Murphy's 'Ramrod', which will kill all emergent annual seedlings over a period of approximately six weeks without harm to other plants.

Nothing, however, is as effective as hoeing as a long-term weed deterrent. This should be a regular procedure once the initial attack has rid the site of the bulk of the weeds. Hoeing has the additional advantage of creating a fine and friable surface mulch which retains soil moisture more effectively than a hard caked surface.

The real crunch comes when weeds like ground elder, bindweed and couch grass get in among the roots of the border plants. Many have such a dense and close-packed root system that it is virtually impossible to separate weeds from plants *in situ* without damage to the latter. When this occurs, and it can happen in an established border that is otherwise weed-free, the only answer is to wait until the plants are dormant. They can then be carefully dug up and planted— always with the minimum of delay—after every scrap of the offending weed has been disentangled from their roots.

DEADHEADING

One of the most important tasks throughout the main season of display is the regular removal of dead flowers. This is an operation that should always be undertaken before the plants have had time to set their seed. There are two good reasons for giving this task a high priority, the first aesthetic, the second more practical. Patches of dead flowers or untidy seedheads can detract from the appearance of the overall display. Some perennials, too, will reward such regular attention with a second burst of bloom. This applies particularly to lupins and delphiniums although there are many other subjects that react in a similar manner. The second batch of blooms is not always as fine as those from the initial flowering, but they help to provide valuable colour when it is most needed late in the season.

I always carry a pair of light secateurs in my back pocket and remove all dead or fading blooms as I go round the garden on my daily tour of inspection. I spare, however, the dead flowers of plants such as *Anemone pulsatilla,* the globe thistle, sea hollies and hellebores, all of which dry well for winter arrangements. And it would be foolish to cut down the flower spikes of that attractive perennial sage, *Salvia superba,* whose bracts remain decorative for many weeks after the flowers have faded.

THINNING

Vigorous growers such as phlox, lupins, delphiniums and michaelmas dasies, will benefit from having the number of shoots reduced by thinning. If all of these are allowed to develop, the quality of the flowers and the vigour of the plants are liable to deteriorate.

Shoots can be thinned in May and June when they are a few inches tall. Up to half their number can be removed, choosing those that are overcrowding the centres of the clumps. Unwanted shoots should be cut off or pinched out as close to soil level as possible.

TIDYING UP

There are two schools of thought concerning the best time for the annual clean-up in the border. Those in favour of a spring clean argue that the dead leaves and stems of the perennials provide winter protection for the crowns. In cold gardens, or in those exposed to strong winds, this could be a factor worth considering. On the other hand, a tangle of dead stems and brown bedraggled foliage is hardly a pretty sight to look at all winter through. Added to this is the fact that such dead vegetation makes ideal winter quarters for a host of pests and diseases. Most gardeners, therefore, will prefer to get their borders shipshape as soon as the last of the michaelmas daisies have made their bow at the end of October.

Any dead stems should be cut right down to ground level. In winter, the stems of many perennials, notably those of michaelmas daisies, phlox, and heleniums, become hard and woody. These have been known to cause serious accidents, since the tips become arrow sharp.

At the same time, the soil between the plants can be forked over lightly—and the operative word is lightly—any remaining weeds being removed in the process. This is a good time to prick in a dressing of well rotted manure or compost. But a newly made border that has had the proper initial preparation, should not need this treatment during its first two or three seasons. Any border, however, will benefit from an early spring dressing of that valuable slow-acting organic fertiliser, bonemeal. It should be applied at the rate of 2-3oz to the sq yd and forked into the top 2in of soil.

DIVISION

Some perennials, as already mentioned, resent disturbance and are best left permanently in the same position. These are usually those with long thonglike tap roots such as peonies. Others, of which michaelmas daisies are a typical example, increase so rapidly that the clumps need breaking up every other year. Plants that sucker divide easily if short lengths of stem, with their accompanying roots, are severed from the parent clump and planted out singly at the distances appropriate to the subject involved.

Others, however, such as phlox and shasta daisies, make such a tight compact root ball that it is virtually impossible to divide them by hand. Two garden forks, back to back, inserted in the clumps and levered apart make such division easy.

CHAPTER SIX

Shrubs with Perennials

Present-day gardening trends favour the use of shrubs in association with perennials. The result is generally referred to as a mixed border. Former champions of the herbaceous border proper would have been horrified by this practice and Gertrude Jekyll and William Robinson must have turned many times in their graves at the thought of such horticultural heresy.

But there is no doubt that the mixed border is a garden feature that has not only come to stay but one that is becoming increasingly popular all the time. For, as well as being labour saving, it extends the interest of the border to the entire twelve months of the year instead of as formerly from about April to the middle or end of October.

This is a factor of no small importance where garden space, as it so often is in the gardens of present-day houses, is restricted almost to the proverbial pocket-handkerchief area, forcing us, willy-nilly into intensive cultivation. This does not mean, however, that all or any kinds of shrubs will make satisfactory bedfellows for perennials.

The mixture will need careful selection, with one kind of plant complementing the other so that all members of the team form an harmonious whole. To achieve this aim, however, is easier said than done and a certain amount of trial and error will be needed before really satisfactory combinations are found.

Points worth bearing in mind when the choice is being made are (1) that the shrubs should not be so large as to dominate the rest of the planting scheme (2) that they should not be voracious soil-robbers and (3) that they do not throw dense shade over too wide an area.

This last problem can often be solved by judicious attention to pruning. The majority of flowering shrubs take kindly to an annual or biennial short-back-and-sides provided that this operation is carried out at the proper time of year.

Among those shrubs that mix especially well with perennials, the old-fashioned rose species and old roses in general hold pride of place. Normally referred to nowadays as 'shrub roses' although all roses are shrubs, these normally do not exceed 6-7ft in height and are easily kept in bounds by light annual pruning.

Shrub roses are easy to cultivate, needing only a minimum of attention. They associate well with almost any kind of border plant. Although, like present-day ramblers, some of the old species and hybrids are single-shot roses with only one flush of bloom occurring around midsummer, this is also true of many other flowering shrubs, in fact of almost all of them. The old roses often compensate generously for this disadvantage by the beauty of their foliage or by the decorative quality of their scarlet heps in autumn.

Others, however, including the hybrid teas and floribundas, offer a continuous display of blossom from June until the end of October and later.

Shrub roses thrive in any good garden soil, although their preference is for a medium loam. Light sandy soils should have plenty of humus added to improve their texture and moisture-retaining qualities.

For the first year or so, newly planted shrub roses will require light pruning to establish a shapely basic framework. Once this aim has been achieved, it will be necessary only to remove some of the old wood each year to encourage the growth of strong new shoots from the base and to cut out any dead or diseased wood that may be present.

One of the earliest of these old fashioned roses to come into flower is 'Canary Bird' a lovely form of the Chinese species *Rosa xanthina*. The scented yellow flowers start to open early in May and effectively complement the blues of lupins and delphiniums.

The yellow blossoms of 'Canary Bird' are closely followed by those of the free flowering 'Fruhlingsgold', the most delightful of the many outstanding hybrids of *R. spinossissima*, the Scots burnet rose. 'Fruhlingsgold' grows up to 7ft tall with elegantly arching stems that are smothered from top to bottom in almost single pale-yellow flowers which turn to a creamy white at maturity. They are very fragrant and their beauty is enhanced by their central cluster of golden stamens.

Another rose species that makes a colourful impact, this time, however, by way of its foliage, is *R. rubrifolia*. The leaves, a deep plum purple, are overlaid with a grey-green bloom. Although the flowers, similar to those of our native dogrose are nothing to rave about, they are followed by deep reddish-brown heps which make a telling contrast to the purple foliage.

R. moyesii and its hybrids are all particularly suitable for the mixed border by reason of the erect and slender habit of growth which lifts their blossom display well above any perennial plants in their vicinity. The flowers are single, like those of an Alexandra rose, and are beautifully set off by the lacy foliage. They are followed by decorative flagon-shaped heps which remain on the bushes until the New Year.

The type plant has flowers of a vivid crimson red with contrasting creamy stamens. 'Geranium' is a more compact form, suitable where space is restricted while 'Sealing Wax' is aptly named for the brilliant lacquer-red colouring of its flowers.

The rugosas are another interesting family of old roses, with varieties that are well worth a place in any mixed border.

Page 71   (right) The so-called 'Ice Plant' *Sedum spectabile;* (below) Agapanthus 'Headbourne Hybrids', the hardiest forms of agapanthus

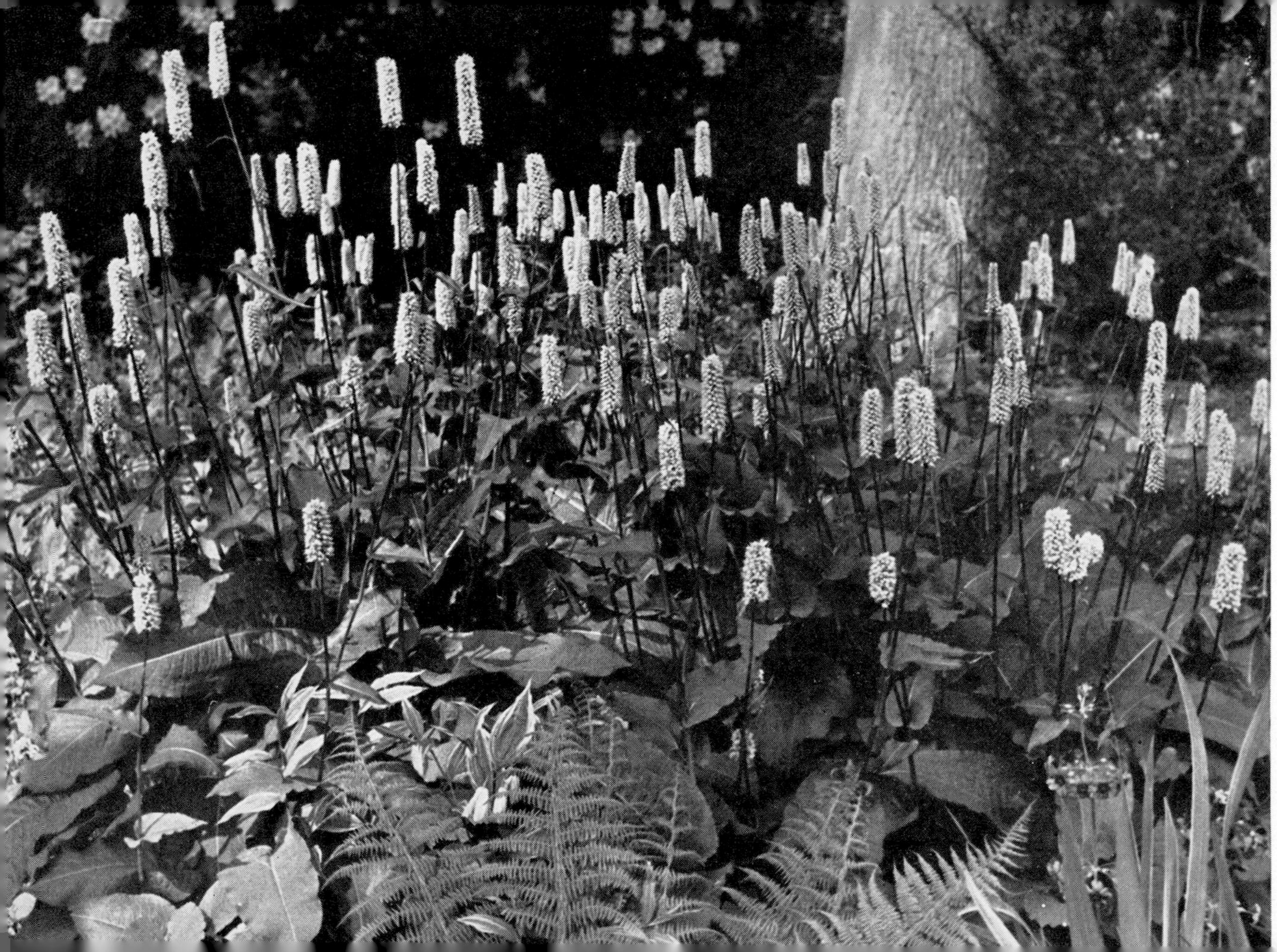

Page 72 *Polygonum bistorta* 'Superbum'

These include some of the shapeliest and most elegant kinds. The rugosas make rounded shrubs with handsome deeply-veined foliage to extend their period of interest throughout the growing season.

One of the loveliest is 'Blanc Double de Coubert' which would take first prize in any whiter-than-white contest. The semi-double blooms, which are especially beautiful at the bud stage, have the appearance of having just been cut out of crinkly crepe paper. Another beauty is 'Frau Dagmar Hastrup' a lovely clear pink rugosa whose blooms have a contrasting centre boss of golden stamens.

Hybrids of *R. rugosa* are well represented by the Grooten-dorst roses, noteworthy for the attractive pinked edges to their petals which makes each bloom look like a miniature picotee carnation. 'Pink Grootendorst' is the brightest star of this par-ticular group.

The Bourbons and China roses have a more continuous-flowering season than those already mentioned. Both groups include numerous worthwhile varieties. One of the loveliest of the Bourbons which would also be my first choice in any collection of these old roses, is the exquisite so-called 'Shell Rose', 'Madame Pierre Oger'. The flowers of this variety are perfect globes, blush pink with incurved petals and an inde-scribably subtle fragrance. This rose flowers from June on-wards and, in mild winters, I have often been able to find one or two almost perfect blooms for the Christmas table.

Also in this group is the better known thornless rose, 'Zephyrine Drouhin'. This is a climber than can be used effectively as a focal point in the border, trained up a stout post or on a metal tripod. The cerise-pink blooms have a scent that is often compared to that of raspberries.

The best known of the China roses is 'Cecile Brunner', a delightful miniature which grows only 2-3ft tall and is ideally suited for a place in the border. The flowers, less than an inch long, are exquisite, exact replicas in miniature of such out-

E

standing hybrid teas as Lady Sylvia, or Madame Butterfly. Given good soil and a place in the sun, Cecile Brunner will flower continuously from June to the beginning of December.

The cult of the 'shrub' rose has given rise to a number of new 'old roses' which are perpetual-flowering and still have all the characteristics of their ancestors. 'Nevada', a hybrid of *R. moyesii,* is one of these. In May and June, every stem is densely clustered with 4in creamy-white blooms. 'Nevada' stages a repeat performance in August on a less grandiose scale and after that continues to flower at intervals during the autumn.

There are also a number of floribundas and various hybrids of recent origin that share many of the virtues of the old roses. At the same time, their vigour and ease of cultivation makes them suitable candidates for a place in the mixed border. An outstanding example is 'Constance Spry', a floribunda that displays all the finest qualities of the old centifolias or cabbage roses, including their delightful fragrance.

'Fritz Nobis' is another that produces masses of flesh-pink HT type blooms that weigh down the branches at midsummer. This rose has a distinctive perfume, like that of the old clove carnations. The flowers are followed by reddish heps. 'Maigold' is a fine golden-yellow hybrid (McGredy's Wonder x Fruhlingsgold) whose parentage is a recommendation of its qualities as a border shrub.

The flowers of 'Maigold' are sweetly scented and the dark glossy foliage makes a perfect foil for their rich golden colouring. It flowers at around midsummer and the flowers are borne over a long period.

Anyone who has tried to restrict that popular floribunda 'Queen Elizabeth' to the same height as other roses in a mixed bed of roses will know that this is virtually impossible. Under normal conditions, an established specimen will reach 8-10ft in a single season.

'Queen Elizabeth' was the first of the so-called 'grandifloras'

—a name used by some rose specialists to describe those floribundas with HT type blooms. Its height and vigour make it an ideal choice for the back of the border. Everyone must, by now, be familiar with the perfectly formed clear-pink blooms of this magnificent rose which are borne, singly at first and then in large clusters.

OTHER SUITABLE SHRUBS

Shrubs which can take regular and fairly drastic pruning are an obvious choice for growing with perennials. They can be kept relatively compact and shapely and will not encroach unduly on the living space of their bedfellows. Many grey and silver-leaved shrubs fall into this category. These, as well as keeping within bounds add considerable interest with their contrasting foliage at all times of the year.

Given a sunny situation and good drainage, all of them are easy to grow and they include artemisias, caryopteris, many of the hebes, or shubby veronicas, lavender, rosemary, olearias and the Russian sage with the almost unpronounceable Latin name, *Perovskia atriplicifolia,* as well as the cotton lavenders or santolinas.

ARTEMISIAS

Everyone must be acquainted with *Artemisia abrotanum* under one of the popular aliases—Lad's Love, southernwood, or Old Man. At one time this aromatic shrub was an established favourite in old cottage gardens. It is fast-growing with lacy grey-green foliage that has a tangy fragrance when crushed or brushed against.

A. arborescens is a smaller and more compact species with a rounded shape and a filigree of fine silver foliage. The outstanding member of the artemisia family is, however, *A. absinthum* 'Lambrook Silver' which originated in the late Mrs Margery Fish's famous garden at Lambrook Manor in Somerset. 'Lambrook Silver' grows only 3-4ft tall with a wide and spreading habit. Its magnificent silver-grey foliage and tremendous vigour make this a shrub worthy of inclusion in any mixed border.

All these artemesias should have their previous year's growth cut right back to its point of origin each spring. This not only helps to maintain their vigour, but keeps the plants compact and shapely.

Incidentally, there are also several useful perennial artemisias that make good border plants. *A. lactiflora,* which grows 5ft tall, is an ideal plant for the shadier parts of the border. In spite of their height, the erect stems never need staking and will stand up to the fiercest of summer gales. It is a plant, too, that knows its place, forming a compact clump that seldom requires division. From July to October *A. lactiflora* bears plumes of creamy-white blossom with the delicate scent of meadowsweet.

'Silver Queen' is a more compact variety, growing only 2ft tall. Its name aptly describes the delicate silvered foliage.

CARYOPTERIS

Caryopteris x *clandonensis,* sometimes referred to as the blue spiraea, is among the most useful flowering shrubs of late summer and early autumn. The foliage, of a pleasing sage grey complements the soft violet blue of the flowers to perfection. This is another shrub that needs really hard pruning each spring to keep it neat and compact.

Since this attractive hybrid appeared in the garden of a former secretary of the Royal Horticultural Society, several others, claiming to be an improvement on the original have made an appearance. 'Ferndown', a seedling from *clandonensis,* has flowers of a deeper blue, as also have 'Kew Blue', another comparatively new introduction, and 'Heavenly Blue'—an American introduction which is more compact in habit than those already mentioned.

PEROVSKIA ATRIPLICIFOLIA

Another worthwhile late summer shrub is the Russian sage, *Perovskia atriplicifolia*. Russian is something of a misnomer since the shrub is native of the Himalayas, but it justifies the second part of its name by the distinctly sage-like aroma of its finely-cut grey leaves. These are borne on tall stems that are felted with a silvery-white down. In August and September, these 6ft stems bear masses of powder-blue flowers. The best variety is 'Blue Spire', with more impressive flowers than the type. It succeeds best in full sun and a particularly fine planting of this interesting shrub can be seen edging the wall of the lodge, just inside the entrance to Wisley Gardens, Surrey.

Incidentally, several of the ornamental forms of the culinary sage, *Salvia officinalis*, make excellent plants for the front of the border. These small shrubs, which are evergreen are grown primarily for the beauty of their dull matt foliage; *S.o.* 'Purpurascens' has leaves of a soft purple and three or four plants will make a striking and permanent splash of colour. 'Tricolor,' as its name implies has grey-green leaves mottled with cream pink and purple. *S.o.* 'Icterina' has leaves that are an interesting medley of green and gold. Pinching back the leaves of these shrubby sages during the growing season will preserve a compact and bushy habit of growth.

Lavender and rosemary are two more herbs, too well known to require description. There are, however, out of the ordinary varieties of each that are more interesting to grow than the commoner ones. I am especially fond of 'Loddon Pink', a delightful pink variety of the fragrant old English lavender, *Lavandula spica*, and I also grow the unusual white variety, *alba*. Where clean, cool fragrance is concerned, there is nothing to choose between these and the purple forms, but they are far more attractive in the mixed border.

There are, as well, several variations on the common rosemary, *Rosmarinus officinalis*. One of these, whose correct name is 'Fastigiata,' is better known as Miss Jessop's variety.

This has a more upright habit of growth than that of the type, which has a tendency to sprawl. Another, which is slightly tender, but which strikes easily from cuttings to provide young plants that can be overwintered in a greenhouse or frame is *R. lavandulaceus* a prostrate species that makes a dense carpet, studded with blue flowers in May and June. It also provides effective weed cover.

SANTOLINAS

In spite of its popular name of cotton lavender, santolina is not related to lavender proper. It is, in fact, a member of the compositae group, with small yellow daisy-like flowers. The santolinas are prized for the lacy effect of their silver-grey foliage as well as for their compact habit of growth. All need a sunny position in well drained soil.

S. chamaecyparissus (*S. incana*) is the best known species, with narrow silver leaves whose edges are serrated. This grows about 2½ft tall and never gets straggly if it is cut back practically to ground level each spring. *Nana* is a dwarf form only a foot in height and makes an ideal subject in groups of six or more at the edge of the border.

S. neapolitana has a looser, more feathery habit of growth than the former while *S. virens* is the odd man out in having foliage of a rich green instead of silver grey.

RUE

Rue is another medicinal and culinary herb which has varieties that function as attractive small border shrubs. *Ruta graveolens* is no taller than the average middle-of-the-border perennial and can be kept short and bushy by annual pruning. 'Jackman's Blue' is a superb garden form with glaucous-blue evergreen foliage that makes a striking impact against summer flower colours and continues to provide interest in winter. I grow, as well, a variety with creamy-white variegation that I find only slightly less attractive than the former.

Rue likes a light, sandy soil—although it seems to do well in my medium loam—and a position in full sun.

OLEARIA

One of my gardening friends, whose Latin pronunciation I am too polite to correct, calls these shrubs O'learyas, I suppose under the mistaken impression they were introduced by an Irishman of the name of O'Leary. In actual fact, the first two syllables are pronounced like the Spanish 'Ole' and the best-known species, *Olearia haastii* was sent to Kew in the middle of last century by a German geologist, Julius Haast, after whom this useful grey-leaved shrub is named. *O. haastii* is completely hardy in Britain but, as might be expected from their Australian origins, most of the other daisy bushes are on the tender side.

O. haastii is widely grown in seaside districts because of its resistance to high winds and salt spray, but its attractive foliage, green above and felted with silver on the underside, makes it a worthwhile shrub for any part of the country. In July and August it is smothered with daisy-like flowers which Alice Coats in her book *Garden Shrubs and Their Histories*, cuttingly but justifiably describes as having 'the greyish look of inadequate laundering'.

This shrub, however, has many compensating characteristics. It is, for instance, highly tolerant of town conditions and happily shrugs off smog and other kinds of atmospheric pollution.

O. macrodonta is more attractive, but will not survive many degrees of frost. It is sometimes known as the New Zealand holly, from the resemblance—in form only—of its felted grey-green leaves to those of our prickly native plant. Like *haastii*, it bears masses of white daisy flowers in July and August and is one of the finest of all shrubs for seaside planting. Both species can be cut back quite hard in spring as soon as they show signs of becoming lank and straggly.

NAME	DESCRIPTION	HEIGHT & SPREAD IN FT.	FLOWERING PERIOD
Abelia grandiflora	Compact bush with sprays of pink flowers	6 x 6	July - September
Aucuba japonica rotundifolia	Compact form of the Japanese laurel. Male and female forms must both be planted for scarlet berries.	2½ x 3½	Autumn berries
Berberis in variety	There are many compact barberries both deciduous and evergreen distinguished for their leaves, flowers and/or berries.	various	April - May
Buddleia fallowiana 'Lochinch'	The most compact of the 'butterfly bushes'. Pale lavender flower spikes, silver-felted leaves	4 x 6	July - September
Ceratostigma willmottianum (False Plumbago)	Useful late summer sub-shrub. Clusters of slate-blue flowers followed by decorative cinnamon seedheads.	3 x 4	July - October
Corokia cotoneaster (Wire netting bush)	Wire-thin twisted branches are responsible for the popular name of this shrub. Tiny oval leaves and yellow star-flowers.	6 x 5	May
Cotoneasters in variety	Many dwarf and creeping forms of this useful family of berried shrubs.	various	Autumn and winter berries
Cytisus praecox (Warminster Broom)	Dwarf brooms with cascades of creamy-yellow flowers in spring.	5 x 6	April - May
Daphnes in variety	All the daphnes are compact with intensely fragrant flowers.	various	January - May
Euphorbia wulfeni (Spurge)	Flue-brush heads of lime-green flowers. Dark evergreen foliage.	3½ x 7	March - May
Forsythia ovata 'Tetragold'	The best compact form of this useful spring-flowering shrub for the border.	4 x 5	February - March
Fuchsias in variety	Many of the hardy fuchsias make fine border plants. Protect in winter with covering of soil or weathered ashes.	various	July - October
Helichrysum serotinum (syn H. angustifolium) (Curry Plant)	Small silver-leaved shrub whose leaves have aroma of curry powder. Flowers yellow.	2½ x 3	July

Name	Description	Size	Flowering
Hypericums in variety	Useful low-growing shrubs with golden chalice flowers. 'Gold Cup' and 'Hidcote' are two outstanding forms.	up to 5 x 7	July - August
Mahonia japonica	Magnificent hollylike evergreen foliage and long racemes of pale yellow, lily-of-the-valley scented flowers.	5 x 8	February - March
Pachysandra terminalis (Japanese spurge)	Evergreen creeping shrub. Good ground cover for a shady border.	½ x indefinite	—
Phlomis fruticosa (Jerusalem sage)	Ever-grey felted leaves and spikes of yellow deadnettle flowers Cut back after flowering.	3½ x 5	June - July
Phormium tenax (New Zealand flax)	Striking broadsword leaves. 6ft spikes of bronzy-red flowers. Bronze-leaved and variegated forms are particularly fine.	6 x 10	July - August
Potentillas in variety	Compact shrubs with small strawberry-like flowers. Exceptionally long flowering season. Cut almost to ground level in spring.	various up to 5 x 7	June - October
Ribes sanguineum (Flowering currant)	One of the earliest and showiest of spring-flowering shrubs. Good forms include 'China Rose', 'King Edward VII' and 'Pulborough Scarlet'	8 x 10	March - April
Romneya x trichocalyx (Californian tree poppy)	Beautiful white satin-petalled poppy-like flowers with striking orange stamens. Prune to base each April.	7 x indefinite	July - October
Spiraea arguta 'Bridal Wreath'	Shapely spring-flowering shrub whose stems are densely festooned with clusters of pure white blossom.	6 x 8	April - May
Spiraea x bumalda 'Anthony Waterer'	Very compact shrub with flat heads of carmine flowers.	4 x 5	June - August
Viburnum davidii	Superb evergreen shrub for edge of border. Oval leaves deeply etched with darker veins.	3 x 5	—

SENECIOS

Like the olearias, the senecios hail from Australasia and share the former's shortcomings—their dislike of sub-zero temperatures—and virtues—a high resistance to wind and exposure. *Senecio laxifolius* and *S. greyii* both grey leaved with yellow daisy flowers are the two hardiest species, but neither is really suited for very cold inland districts.

S. cineraria, formerly known as *Cineraria maritima,* is possibly the finest of all silver-leaved shrubs. The foliage is lacy and deeply incised. It has a low spreading habit of growth that makes it an ideal choice for the edge of the border. *S. cineraria* is not only tender but also susceptible to wet. It has, however, survived numerous winters in my garden, at the foot of a south wall in near-drought conditions. I grow the variety White Diamond which is considered to be a great improvement on the type and take a few cuttings for over-wintering under glass in case of complete losses out of doors. Pinching back the main shoots in summer checks its tendency to straggle.

The shrubs discussed above form only a small proportion of those suitable for associating with perennials. The appended list gives details in brief of others that are similarly useful.

CHAPTER SEVEN

The Year in the Border

Although a herbaceous border is primarily a summer and autumn feature, there is no reason why it should not provide more continuing interest, albeit in a more restricted manner, throughout the rest of the year, especially if shrubs, bulbs, corms and tubers are used to supplement the rather sparse display from perennials at these times.

With the possible exception of really hard winters, there should be something to tempt us into the garden on every day of the year. The brilliant purples of the winter heaths, for example, glow all the more brightly against a background of snow while shrubs like witch hazel, *Viburnum fragrans* and the yellow winter jasmine are very little deterred from flowering by sub-zero weather conditions.

Such winters, fortunately, are comparatively exceptional in most parts of the country and we hope to enjoy the beauty of isolated patches of colour all through the winter, beginning in November, when most border perennials start to hibernate, until the beginning of April, when flowers start to appear again in quantity.

Among the first perennials to come into flower in winter are the hellebores. Of these, the Christmas rose, *H. niger,* is the best known species. but there are many others described in detail in Chapter 4, that will provide continuity of colour and interest from November to May.

Another perennial that should be in flower at Christmas is

83

the winter iris, *Iris unguicularis* (syn *I. stylosa*). The scented lilac flowers, cowering in an untidy cluster of rushlike foliage, look far too delicate to survive the merest touch of frost but they are actually as tough as old boots and continue to appear in batches during any sunny spells from November to February. Picked in bud, the flowers will open indoors and last for several days.

The winter iris does best in really poor dry soil, in full sunlight. The previous year's foliage can be cut right back in April, to keep the clumps tidy. The plants may take several years to develop their full flowering potential. In addition to the ordinary form, there is a white variety 'Alba' and one with flowers of a richer purple, 'Mary Barnard'.

Arum italicum marmoratum is closely related to our native cuckoopint. It is grown for the beauty of its leaves with their marbled green and cream variegation and their unusual spear shape. These begin to appear in late autumn soon after the rather uninteresting green arum-like flowers have faded.

Winter-flowering pansies are easy to raise from seed sown out of doors or in cold frames in early June. They will start to flower in autumn and continue right through to the following summer if the winter is comparatively mild. In colder seasons, they will call a halt and come into bloom again in March. Seed is obtainable in colourful mixtures or in separate colours that include blue, yellow and white.

Primroses and polyanthus are both members of another group of plants that give an early display. Primroses, now obtainable in strains of superb mixed colours, will begin flowering in February, reaching their peak performance in March and April. Polyanthus are a few weeks later in flowering and continue until the end of May.

The seeds of primroses and polyanthus germinate slowly and erratically. Sowings should be made in a cold greenhouse or frame from March to June. The best flowering plants for the following season will be obtained from the earlier sowings.

As soon as the seedlings are large enough to handle, they should be pricked off into boxes or into a cold frame. Later, they can go out into a nursery bed, prior to planting out in their permanent positions in September or October.

Although the giant-flowered strains are superb, with individual flowers as much as 2in across, it is better to use the more ordinary strains for planting in the open border. These are hardier and more resistant to wind and weather.

Polyanthus and primroses will grow either in sun or shade. In sunny situations, however, they should have soil that is rich in humus and retentive of moisture. Good strains of coloured primroses include Suttons' Colour Magic and Dobies' Mothers Day. Suttons' giant strain of polyanthus or Dobies' superb mixed are both outstandingly good for border planting.

Another useful member of the primula family for an early spring show is the drumstick primula, *Primula denticulata.* This has large globular blooms on 12in stems rising from a rosette of fine green foliage. The seed of these can be sown in May or June and treated in a similar manner to those of primrose or polyanthus to provide flowering plants for the following spring. The flowers of the type plant are mauve, but there are also other colours in various shades of lavender and rich purple, as well as white.

In April, clumps of the dogs-tooth violet, *Erythronium dens-canis* can be one of the loveliest sights in the border. There is something vaguely oriental in the appearance of the nodding stellate flowers. Those of the common form are lilac; there are also many other varieties and hybrids in delightful shades of pink, purple and white.

The epimediums or barrenworts, are relations of the barberries. These form another group of early flowering perennials, with heart-shaped leaves, delicately veined and tinted with bronze in most species. They flower in April and the leaves colour attractively in autumn. The delicate sprays of bloom are borne on stems like finely drawn wire.

The creeping rootstocks of these plants although never aggressively invasive, successfully inhibit weed growth. *E. macranthum* 'Rose Queen' has rosy-purple flowers. The more compact *E. warleyensis* has spikes of orange-red blooms.

E. pinnatum is slightly taller than either of these at 15in, with bright yellow flowers, while *E. youngii niveum* has white flowers set off by foliage of a pale apple green. This persists throughout the winter and should be cut back to ground level each February, before the new leaves appear.

Towards the end of April, with the coming of longer and warmer days, the border display begins in earnest, rising to its zenith in July and August and continuing until mid-October, or, in favoured conditions and mild seasons, well into November.

The list that follows describes many of these plants in detail, giving, wherever applicable, the approximate flowering period for the southern half of the British Isles. In northern England and Scotland, flowering may sometimes begin and finish a fortnight or so in advance of this. Dates can, in any case, very considerably from district to district and according to soil and climatic conditions and season.

The figures in brackets show the average height of the plants mentioned.

ACANTHUS
See Chapter 4 pp 49-50

ACHILLEA (MILFOIL)   Sun

The achilleas are sun-loving plants which have finely cut fernlike foliage which is aromatic when crushed. The flower heads, of great architectural value in the border, are flat and platelike in character. The tallest form is *Achilea filipendulina* 'Gold Plate' with grey-green foliage. The yellow flowers are borne on erect 5ft stems.

'Moonshine' (2) is a more compact variety with pale yellow flowers and attractive silvery foliage. 'Coronation Gold' (3) is an intermediate form with bright yellow flowers. There are also two more out of the ordinary forms, 'Fire King' and 'Cerise Queen' whose flower heads are crimson and cerise respectively. The flat heads, picked when fully open, dry well for winter arrangements.

Achillea ptarmica 'The Pearl' has clusters of double pure white button flowers that are valued for cutting. They associate well with roses or sweet peas in formal arrangements.
Flowering period June - July

ALCHEMILLA (Lady's Mantle)   Sun
Alchemilla mollis (2) is one of the best ground cover plants extremely attractive in its own right with rounded pale-green silken-textured leaves each of which, after summer showers, will hold a raindrop, like a jewel, at its centre. The yellowish-green flowers are borne in loose clusters. *A. mollis* seeds freely, perhaps too freely for all tastes.
Flowering period June - August

ANAPHALIS   Sun
These are silver-foliaged plants which bear clusters of papery greyish-white 'everlasting' flowers. They make ideal subjects for a grey and silver border.
Anaphalis triplinervis (1) is a dwarf form suitable for the edge of the border. *A. yedoensis* (3) is taller, with flowers more loosely borne on tall stems.
Flowering period July - August

ANCHUSA   Sun
These members of the borage family are very susceptible to cold damp conditions and therefore do best on light sandy soils. Spring planting is essential. Anchusas have flowers of an intense sky blue. Good named forms include 'Loddon Royal-

ist' (3) with royal-blue flowers; 'Morning Glory' (4) gentian-
blue and 'Opal' (4) Cambridge blue. 'Little John' (1½) is a
dwarf form with rich blue flowers and a long flowering season.
Flowering period June - August

ANEMONE HYBRIDA (Japanese Anemone)   Sun or Shade
   The Japanese anemones are among the most useful late-
blooming perennials with a long flowering season. They have
pink or white saucer-shaped flowers 2½in across held proudly
above attractively cut foliage. They are plants that should
not be disturbed once established. 'Profusion' (2½) reddish-
pink, 'September Charm' (2) pink, Bressingham Glow' (1½)
a compact and semi-double rosy-crimson form and 'Louise
Uhink' (3), a semi-double white, are among the finest named
forms.
Flowering period August - October

ANTHEMIS TINCTORIA (Dyer's Greenweed)   Sun
   The yellow daisy flowers which are borne in profusion are
good for cutting. Anthemis need a well-drained soil. 'Beauty
of Grallach' (2-3) has deep golden-yellow flowers, 'Mrs E. C.
Buxton' (2½) is a pale lemon yellow and 'Sancta Johannis'
(2) is orange yellow.
Flowering period July - August

AQUILEGIA (Columbine)   Sun or Part Shade
   Aquilegias do best when raised afresh from seed each year
and treated as biennials although a number of named forms
are offered by nurserymen. They are valuable May-flowering
border plants with attractive maidenhair-like foliage and
spurred bonnet flowers. 'Crimson Star' (2), crimson and white,
'McKana hybrids', a strain of longspurred aquilegias in a wide
range of colours and A. glandulosa (1) a dwarf blue and white
columbine are all named forms worth growing.
Flowering period May - June

Page 89 (right) *Anemone x hybrida* 'September Charm'; (below) *Rudbeckia fulgida deamii* commonly known as 'Black-eyed Susan'

Page 90 (above) *Solidago* 'Golden Thumb', a fine dwarf form of goldenrod for edging; (right) *Echinops ritro* 'Taplow Blue'. A good named form of the globe thistle

ASTILBE   Sun or Shade

The astilbes are a race of moisture and shade-loving plants that will, nevertheless, succeed in full sun provided they are given plentiful supplies of water and humus during the summer. Their ferny foliage is as attractive as the frothy plumes of blossom. In many varieties, too, the leaves are a striking bronzy red when they first unfurl in spring. Of the taller growing varieties, 'Betsy Cuperus' with pale shell-pink plumes and 'Salland', deep lilac-rose are both good. They both grow 3½ft tall. The remaining varieties, all in the 2-2½ft range, include 'Federsee', bright rosy crimson, 'Finale', clear pink and flowering some weeks later than the others, and not to be confused with 'Fanal', whose flowers are a dark turkey red, 'William Reeves', crimson scarlet and the beautiful snow white 'Irrlicht'.

Flowering period July - August

BERGENIA   Sun or Shade
See Chapter 3, pp 45-6

BRUNNERA MACROPHYLLA (Giant Forget-me-not)
                                                      Sun or Part Shade

This is a fine early-flowering perennial, 1½ft in height whose large soft-green leaves make first-class ground cover. It bears sprays of rich blue forget-me-not flowers.

Flowering period April - June

CAMPANULA (Bellflower)   Sun or Part Shade

The campanulas are a race of summer-flowering perennials whose value in the border cannot be over stressed. They have a liking for rich moist soil conditions. These are the best species:

C. burghaltii (2) This is an unusual species that should be better known. It bears large numbers of long lilac-grey bells of great beauty.

F

C. glomerata (1¼) This species bears dense clusters of violet-blue flowers, spherical in shape and rather like the blooms of a ponticum rhododenron.

C. lactiflora (4-5) The type plant has tall spikes of pale blue bellflowers. 'Loddon Anna', with lilac-pink flowers is a good variety to grow.

C. latifolia (4) (Giant Bellflower) This is one of the better species, with large long bells of great beauty and magnificent form. 'Alba', white and 'Brantwood', violet-purple are two good forms.

In addition to these there are a number of dwarf species and varieties of campanula that are normally included in the alpine and rock plant section of nurserymen's catalogues. Two of the best known of these are *C. carpatica* (½) with hare-bell flowers in violet, white or pink and *C. portenschlagiana* with masses of pale purple bells. This grows only 4in tall but makes up for this in spread and beauty of blossom. Both these dwarf forms are useful for grouping at the front of the border to provide colour over a long period.

Flowering period June - August

CATANANCHE COERULEA (Cupid's Dart)   Sun

Catananche coerulea major (3) a delightful plant with corn-flower-type flowers backed with silvery bracts, borne on very long stems which makes it good for cutting. It likes dry conditions and does not tolerate very wet winters. It has a long flowering period.

Flowering period June - September

CHRYSANTHEMUM MAXIMUM (Shasta Daisy)   Sun

These rampant perennials may be somewhat over vigorous for the smaller herbaceous border, where the space they occupy could be used for choicer subjects. Where space is available, however, their large white daisy-flowers can be very attractive. These cut and last well. Good varieties include

'Everest' and 'Jennifer Read', both singles with a yellow 'button' and doubles such as 'Esther Read', 'Horace Read' and 'John Murray'. They average 2½-3ft in height.
Flowering period June - August

CIMICIFUGA (Bugwort)   Sun or Part Shade
The cimicifugas are a race of elegant foliage plants with long narrow plumes of creamy-white flowers on tall stems. They have a distinct preference for moist soil conditions. Species and varieties are as follows:
C. cordifolia (4) This species has tapering flower spikes borne above finely-cut lacy foliage.
C. racemosa (6) A superb subject for planting at the back of the border. It has slender arching spikes of creamy blossom, a foot or more in length.
C. simplex 'White Pearl' (3) This is a more compact version with similar characteristics of flowers and foliage.
Flowering period July - August

COREOPSIS   Sun
These perennials, with their golden-yellow daisy-like flowers have a phenomenally long flowering period. *C. grandiflora* (2½) with its rather harsh yellow colouring is sometimes difficult to place in the border. *C. verticillata* makes a much better border plant. It is neat and compact with rich green linear foliage that makes an ideal setting for the dainty 1in yellow flowers.
Flowering period July - September

DELPHINIUM   Sun
See Chapter 3, p 34

CYNOGLOSSUM NERVOSUM (Hound's Tongue)   Sun
Cynoglossum nervosum is a valuable middle of the border plant (2½) with large sprays of intensely blue forget-me-not

flowers and hairy borage-like foliage. It is closely related to
the anchusas
Flowering period June - August

DICENTRA SPECTABILIS (Bleeding Heart)   Sun or Part Shade
   This plant has elegant arching sprays of pendent pink and
white locket-shaped flowers whose curious shape have earned
it the other popular name of 'Dutchman's Breeches'. It is
also found listed as Dielytra. The flowers cut well.
Flowering period April - June

DICTAMNUS FRAXINELLA (Burning Bush)   Sun or Part Shade
   The burning bush has finely-cut, ashlike foliage (1½) and
spikes of pinkish-mauve flowers on erect stems. It gets its
popular name from the fact that, on still summers' nights,
the volatile oils given off by the leaves can be ignited with a
match without harm to the plants.
Flowering period June - August

DORONICUM (Leopardsbane)   Sun
See Chapter 3, pp 46-7

ECHINOPS RITRO (Globe Thistle)   Sun or Part Shade
   These handsome plants, of great architectural value in the
border, have grey-green thistle-like leaves and steel-blue
prickly globular blooms on stiff stems. They dry well for win-
ter arrangements. Good varieties include 'Taplow Blue' (5),
'Blue Ball' (4½) with flowers of a softer blue and a dwarf form
'Veitch's Blue' (2½) with large deep blue flowers.
Flowering period July - August

EPIMEDIUM (Barrenwort)   Sun or Part Shade
See Chapter 7, pp 87-8

EREMURUS (Foxtail Lily)   Sun
   The foxtail lilies make imposing subjects for focal points

of interest. Their massive flower spikes of yellow pink or white are 5-8ft tall and should be protected from wind. Plants can be raised from seed sown in a cold frame in spring to provide material for planting out in autumn. They need rich well-prepared soil. *E. bungei* (5) has golden yellow flowers with orange anthers. *E. robustus* (6-8) has sweetly scented pale pink flowers.
Flowering period May - June

ERYNGIUM (Sea Holly)   Sun
See Chapter 4, pp 50-1

EUPHORBIA (Spurge)   Sun or Part Shade
See Chapter 4, pp 56-60

GERANIUM (Cranesbill)   Sun or Part Shade
The true geraniums, as opposed to the zonal pelargoniums which commonly answer to this name, are hardy perennials which make a fine display in the border and whose clumps of rounded leaves make excellent ground cover.

G. *ibericum* (2) is a vigorous plant which compensates for a relatively short flowering period by the beauty of its dark-green foliage. Good forms include 'Alba', white, 'Flore Pleno', violet-blue and 'Johnson's Blue'.

The smaller species and hybrids have a much longer flowering season. Among the best of these are G. *endressii* 'Wargrave' (2) salmon-pink with grey-green leaves, 'Russell Pritchard' (1½) a prostrate species with sage-green leaves and purple flowers and 'Rose Clair' (2) which produces its pale-pink blooms all through the summer months.
Flowering period May - August

GEUM   Sun
The geums provide brilliant flower colour over a long period and their dense foliage also makes good ground cover.

The old favourites, 'Mrs Bradshaw', double scarlet and 'Lady Stratheden' a semi-double bright yellow are still the most commonly seen kinds. 'Fire Opal' (2) reddish-orange and *borisii*, orange-scarlet are two more good forms.
Flowering period May - August

GYPSOPHILA (Baby's Breath)   Sun
Gypsophila paniculata is a perennial for which a place should be found in any border. The clouds of tiny white flowers, borne in large clusters on thin wiry stems are as useful for cutting as they are acting as a foil for the heavier border flowers.

The common form, 3ft in height, has single flowers. 'Rosy Veil' is more compact with a spreading habit and double pale-pink flowers. 'Pink Star' is an attractive dwarf form, while 'Bristol Fairy' a double white, is considered to be an improvement on the type.

Slugs are very partial to the young shoots of gypsophila. Plants should be ringed with sharp ashes or a sprinkling of slug bait or total losses may be experienced.
Flowering period June - August

HELENIUM   Sun
The daisy flowers of the heleniums, with their prominent central disc, borne in great profusion, make these perennials some of the finest subjects for the summer and autumn display. There are around a dozen good named varieties, ranging in colour from sulphur yellow to deep mahogany red, few of which require staking. Heights range from $2\frac{1}{2}$-4ft and the flowers cut and last well. In some, the central 'button' is in a contrasting colour to the petals.
Varieties:
'Bruno' (3) Deep mahogany with a darker centre.
'Butterpat' (3)—bright yellow.
'Copper Spray' (2)—coppery orange marked with gold.

'Moerheim Beauty' (3)—deep mahogany
'The Bishop' (1½)—deep yellow, with dark brown centre.
'Wyndley' (3)—deep yellow, striped with orange, brown centres.
Flowering period July - September

HELIANTHUS (Perennial Sunflower)   Sun
   Although some of the perennial sunflowers are unduly invasive the following kinds do not share this tendency:
'Loddon Gold' (4)—splendid variety with double yellow flowers 4in across.
'Capenoch Star' (5)—single yellow.
Flowering period August - September

HELLEBORE   Part Shade
See Chapter 4, pp 51-2

HEMEROCALLIS (Day-Lilies)   Sun or Part Shade
See Chapter 4, pp 55-6

HEUCHERA (Alum Root)   Part Shade
   The heucheras make excellent plants for the front of the border. Their clusters of tiny bells on wiry stems, rising from neat rosettes of rounded leaves are delicate and eye catching. 'Red Spangles' (1½) vivid deep red, 'Scintillation' (1½) pink, tipped with carmine, 'Apple Blossom' (2½) pale pink and the even paler 'Lady Romney' (2½) are all good varieties. 'Pearl Drops' (2) is an unusual form with pearly-white flowers on erect dainty stems; 'Coral Cloud' has blossom sprays of a striking coral-red.
   Heucherella 'Bridget Bloom', a bigeneric cross between a heuchera and the foam flower, *Tiarella wherryi* is an even more outstanding border plant. It grows about 1½ft tall and is seldom without flowers from May to late October. The large sprays of bloom are shell-pink in colour.
Flowering period June - September

HOSTA (Plantain Lily)   Sun or Part Shade
See Chapter 4, pp 52-5

IRIS   Sun
See Chapter 3, pp 37-9

KNIPHOFIA (Red-hot Poker)   Sun
The red-hot pokers are among the most popular border
plants. There are quite a few different species and between
them, these provide a succession of bloom throughout summer and autumn. One of the earliest to flower is 'Bee's Sunset' (3) with 'pokers' of a brilliant flame colour. 'Royal Standard' (4) has the typical scarlet-tipped flower spikes that are
responsible for the popular name of this plant. 'Maid of
Orleans' (3) is noteworthy for the beauty of its tall ivory
torches while the species *northiae* (5) forms handsome clumps
of yucca-like foliage topped by cream and coral spikes built
on the same magnificent scale.
Flowering period July - September

LINUM (Perennial Flax)   Sun
The perennial flaxes, none of which grow particularly tall
make fine plants for the front of a sunny border. *Linum perenne* (1) bears a profusion of pale blue flowers on arching
stems. *L. narbonense* (1½), also flowers very freely, the dainty
blue flowers almost smothering the foliage.
There are several dwarf forms not exceeding 6in in height.
L. arboreum is a tiny silver-grey bush with large golden-
yellow flowers and *L. flavum,* a prostrate form has flowers of
a similar colour.
Flowering period June - September

LOBELIA   Sun or Part Shade
Lobelia cardinalis (syn *L. fulgens*) the cardinal flower, is a
rich and sumptuous relation of the popular dwarf blue bed-

ding lobelias, but bears little or no resemblance to them. The brilliant scarlet flowers of this splendid perennial are particularly eye catching in the summer border, while the beetroot-red foliage provides additional colour throughout the season. It is, unfortunately, not complete-hardy and needs winter protection against damp and frost.

Cuttings, taken in spring, root easily and can be over-wintered in a cold frame as an insurance against losses. Spring planting is essential. 'Queen Victoria' and 'The Bishop', both in the region of 3ft are good named forms.

There is a less common form with blue flowers, *L. vedrariensis* (5), with spikes of violet-blue flowers and green foliage. This, too, will need protection in severe winters.
Flowering period July - October

LYCHNIS (Campion)   Sun
Of this race of perennials, the scarlet campion, *Lychnis chalcedonica* (3) is the most commonly seen. It has rounded heads of intensely scarlet small flowers which make a striking contrast to the emerald green of the leaves. *L. coronaria,* the rose campion, is another popular garden plant with cerise flowers and greyish woolly leaves as well as a habit of seeding itself in every part of the garden. It is a plant to be avoided where the herbaceous border is concerned.

L. flos-jove, the flower of Jove, is an attractive early-flowering species with purple or scarlet flowers and grey felted foliage.
Flowering period June - August

LYSIMACHIA (Yellow Loosestrife)   Sun or Part Shade
Lysimachia punctata, a close relation of the cottager's favourite Creeping Jenny and with similar yellow flowers is a useful border plant by reason of needing no staking. Its sturdy 3ft stems bear a golden-yellow flower in each leaf axil. It spreads rather rapidly and its invasive tendencies will need

careful watching. *L. ephereum* (2½) is a much more attractive species, with slender spikes of white flowers above greyish foliage.
Flowering period June - September

LYTHRUM (Purple Loosestrife)   Sun or Part Shade
The purple loosestrife, *L. salicarium* is an easy plant for all types of garden soil. It is useful for providing continuity of colour when the main display is past its peak. Good varieties include 'Robert' (3) rose-pink and 'Brightness' (3) a deeper pink. *L. virgatum* 'Rose Queen' is another well worth growing.
Flowering period July - September

MACLEAYA CORDATA (Plume Poppy)   Sun or Part Shade
The plume poppy is a splendid five-footer for the back of the border, but with somewhat invasive tendencies in rich soils. It has grey-green attractively lobed vinelike leaves and feathery plumes of buff-pink blossom bearing not the slightest resemblance to that of any other poppy. The plume poppy needs little or no staking.
Flowering period August

MONARDA DIDYMA (Bergamot)   Sun or Part Shade
Bergamot is an aromatic herb whose leaves are used to give the distinctive flavour to Earl Grey tea. The flowers, which are borne in clusters are small and tubular. The plants form a dense mat of roots but top growth disappears almost completely during winter and care must be taken not to disturb them when the border is receiving its annual tidy-up. The monardas have a preference for fairly rich soil conditions.
Varieties:
'Cambridge Scarlet' (2½)—brilliant scarlet
'Croftway Pink' (2½)—lilac pink
'Blue Stocking' (2½)—violet purple

'Snow Maiden' (2½)—white
Flowering period July - September

NEPETA (Catmint) Sun

These sun-loving plants have grey aromatic foliage and produce their lavender-mauve flower spikes over a very long period. The common form *Nepeta mussinii* (1) makes a first class edging plant; the variety 'Six Hills Giant' (2½) is more impressive, with longer violet spikes and dark grey foliage. Catmint does best in light sandy soils. In heavy damp clays it does not always survive the winter.
Flowering period June - August

PEONY Sun or Part Shade
See Chapter 3, pp 41-4

PAPAVER ORIENTALE (Oriental poppy) Sun

The oriental poppy is a showy but somewhat untidy plant, since the stems keel over into a sprawling mess as soon as the plants have finished flowering. The large black-centred poppy flowers, whose petals look as though they have been cut out of crêpe paper are 3-4in across.

Oriental poppies are easily raised from seed. Sowings in early summer will produce plants to flower the following season. Good named forms include 'Marcus Perry' (orange scarlet), 'Mary Sadler (salmon pink) 'Ethel Swete' (deep rosy red) and 'Perry's White'. All grow to a height of 2½-3ft.
Flowering season May - June

PENSTEMON Sun or Part Shade
Penstemons have attractive tubular flowers that they display the length of erect stems. Their exceptionally long flowering season makes them valuable subjects for the border. *Penstemon barbatus* (Bearded Tongue) has bright scarlet flowers on 4-5ft stems. *P. hartwegii* 'Firebird' is shorter

(1½-2) with flowers of a deeper scarlet. Penstemons should be planted in spring.
Flowering season July - October

PHLOX   Sun or Part Shade
See Chapter 3, pp 39-41

PHYSALIS FRANCHETTI (Chinese Lantern Plant or
    Cape Gooseberry)   Sun or Part Shade
    Fast spreading and invasive perennials with white potato-like flowers that are followed by scarlet papery 'lanterns', enclosing a cherry-like fruit. Excellent dried for winter decoration.
Flowering period July - August

PHYSOSTEGIA VIRGINIANA (Obedient Plant) Sun or Part Shade
    As well as being an extremely useful subject for providing autumn colour with its spikes of lilac-pink flowers, the obedient plant is something of an horticultural curiosity. Each of the individual florets on the flower spikes is on a sort of ball and socket joint which enables it to stay put in whichever direction it is moved. In addition to the type plant there is a white form 'Summer Snow' and 'Vivid', with brilliant rose-pink flowers. All varieties are between 2 and 2½ft in height.
Flowering period September - October

PULMONARIA (Lungwort)   Part or Full Shade
See Chapter 3, p 47

PYRETHRUM   Sun
    These popular daisy-flowered perennials start to flower in May and will continue right through to August provided faded flower stems are cut right back to soil level. Pyrethrums need soil that is rich in humus and should be planted out in spring.

Varieties:
'Avalanche'—white
'Brenda'—single cerise pink. A vigorous variety
'Eileen May Robinson'—salmon pink single
'Progression'—double flowers of pale rose
'Scarlet Glow'—single crimson scarlet
All the above grow to a height of about 2ft
Flowering period May - August

RUDBECKIA (Coneflower)   Sun or Part Shade
The rudbeckias bear a profusion of yellow daisy flowers in late summer. They do best in good soil and in a position in full sun but will also tolerate a certain amount of shade. The flowers of some varieties have a contrasting central disc of green, black or brown.
Varieties:
'Autumn Sun' (Herbstsonne)—yellow flowers with raised central green cone (6)
'Goldsturm'—long-petalled yellow daisies with large black central disc (2)
'Newmannii speciosa'—masses of yellow, black-centred daisies on branching stems. Sometimes known as Black-eyed Susan, a name it shares with the half-hardy annual, *Thunbergia alata* (2).
Flowering period July - September

SALVIA (Sage)   Sun
The perennial sages have attractive spikes of blue or violet flowers and are free flowering. The finest border form is, without doubt, S. *superba* (S. *virgata nemorosa*) (2½) which has long violet spikes whose cinnamon-brown bracts continue to provide decorative value long after the flowers have faded. S. *haematodes* (3) is a species with elegant branching spikes of lavender flowers while the taller S. *uliginosa* (5) flowers in autumn to brighten the border with its spikes of gentian-blue flowers.

Flowering period July - August
S. uliginosa August - September

SCABIOUS   Sun
Scabious are lime-loving plants with an exceptionally long flowering season. They are excellent for cutting and need no staking. They should be planted out in spring. Hybrid strains in a mixture of colours are easily raised from seed.
Named varieties:
'Clive Greaves' (3)—lavender-blue flowers on tall stems
'Miss Willmott' (3)—a white counterpart of the above
Flowering period June - October

SEDUM (Stonecrop)   Sun
The border stonecrops are a race of interesting succulent plants with fleshy glaucous foliage and rounded heads of small flowers which appear late in the summer and attract the bees and butterflies in the same way as the blossoms of *Buddleia davidii*. *Sedum spectabile* is the species most widely grown and is sometimes known as the 'ice plant'. 'Meteor' (1½) is the best variety with very large heads of rose-coloured flowers on sturdy stems.
There are also some striking newer hybrids, including 'Autumn Joy' (2½) with enormous heads of dusky pink flowers and 'Ruby Glow' (1) a more compact plant with bluish-purple leaves and small heads of ruby-red flowers.
Flowering period August - October

SIDALCEA   Sun
The sidalceas are easy to grow in any soil conditions. They have mallowlike flowers borne on upright stems.
Varieties:
'Rose Queen' (3)—rose-pink flowers
'Rev Page Roberts' (4)—paler pink flowers
'Crimson King' (3)—ruby red

'Mrs Alderson' (4)—an old favourite with large clear pink flowers.
Flowering period July - August

SOLIDAGO (Goldenrod)   Sun or Part Shade
The goldenrods are another group of perennials eminently useful for the late display. Unlike the older spreading kinds, the newer forms are compact and need no staking. The flowers are yellow and are borne in fluffy, mimosa-like sprays. They associate well with michaelmas daisies and share their flowering season.
Varieties:
'Goldenmosa' (3)—the golden-yellow flowers of this variety have a powdered appearance like those of mimosa.
'Golden Wings' (5)—a taller variety with golden plumes that spread out laterally.
'Lemore' (1½)—this is a good dwarf form for the edge of the border. It has sprays of lemon-yellow flowers.
'Loddon Gold' (3)—slender spikes of deep yellow flowers.
Flowering period August - September

STACHYS LANATA (Lamb's Ears)   Sun
This is a fine foliage plant with thickly-felted grey woolly leaves that hug the ground and make a dense weed-smothering mat. The ordinary form has 2ft spikes of insignificant purple flowers. 'Silver Carpet' (4in) which does not flower, is a much better form for edging and carpeting.
Flowering period June - July

SYMPHITUM (Comfrey)   Shade
This is a race of perennials that should be better known, since the symphitums will provide attractive flowers in the shadier parts of the border during early spring. They are tolerant of poor soil conditions and will even thrive under trees. The flowers are tubular and hang down in clusters from erect stems.

S. caucasicum (2) is the earliest to flower with deep blue flowers in April and May.

S. grandiflorum (1) makes a good carpeter. The flowers are pale yellow.

S. peregrinum (3)—clear blue flowers, reddish-brown in bud. There is also a variety with silver-variegated foliage and blue flowers—*S. officinale* 'Argenteum'

Flowering period April - July

THALICTRUM (Meadow Rue)   Sun or Part Shade

The meadow rues have lacy foliage rather like that of an outsize maidenhair fern. The flowers are borne in loose clusters.

Garden species include:

T. dipterocarpum (5-6)—a fine plant for the back row of the border with masses of small lavender flowers.

T. aquilegium (2½)—a dwarf species with grey-green foliage and rosy-purple heads of bloom.

T. glaucum (5) is the best foliage species. The leaves are a striking glaucous blue and it bears rounded heads of yellow flowers.

Flowering period June - August

TIARELLA CORDIFOLIA (Foam Flower)   Part or Full Shade

The foam flower, which grows about 9in tall, makes an ideal carpeting plant for the shadier edges of the border. The heart-shaped leaves are evergreen and smother weeds effectively. Bears masses of frothy cream bottle-brush flower spikes.

Flowering period June

TRADESCANTIA (Spiderwort)   Sun or Part Shade

The spiderworts are noteworthy for their neat and attractive rush-like foliage and for their exceptionally long flowering period. The three-petalled flowers open deep down in the centre of the leaf clumps.

Page 107 (above) *Anaphalis yedoensis* One of the best of the grey-leaved perennials; (below) *Artemisia gnapalodes* A perennial species of artemisia, grown for the beauty of its silver-grey foliage

Page 108 (left) *Perovskia atriplici-folia,* the Russian Sage, provides colour in the border late in the season; (below) *Phalaris arundinacea* 'Picta', one of the best of the variegated ornamental grasses

Good varieties include:
'J. C. Weguelin' (2) wedgwood blue, 'Taplow Crimson' (1½) crimson-red, 'Kreisler' (2) gentian-blue, 'Isis' (1½) mid-blue and 'Purple Dome' (1½) rich violet.
Flowering period June - October

TROLLIUS (Globe Flower)   Sun or Part Shade
   The globe flower is a close relation of the buttercup. Its spherical, fully double flowers provide welcome splashes of yellow in the early summer border. *T. europaeus,* the wild form makes an attractive garden plant but varieties such as 'Canary Bird' (2½), clear yellow, 'Golden Queen' (2½) brilliant orange, 'Alabaster' (1½) creamy-yellow and 'Orange Princess' (1½) deep yellow, are all a good deal showier than the type.
Flowering period May - July

VERONICA (Speedwell)   Sun or Part Shade
   There are many different species of veronica and *V. gentianoides* (2) is one of the most attractive, with slender flower spikes of gentian-blue in May. Most other species flower later, including 'Barcarolle' (1½) with rose-pink flowers, 'Royal Blue' (1½) gentian-blue. There are several forms of more prostrate habit that make attractive edging plants. These include *V. prostrata* (3in) with blue flowers on short spikes, 'Shirley Blue' (1) which is semi-prostrate and 'Spode Blue', a compact form smothered in china-blue spikes.
Flowering period June - August

G

CHAPTER EIGHT

Bulbs, Corms and Tubers

Many bulbous plants—and in this category, for convenience sake, I include corms such as gladioli and tubers like begonias —associate well with perennials and are of great help in supplementing and extending the display. Among the first to make their contribution are the winter aconites, which are tuberous rooted. They open their golden buttercup flowers, each surrounded by a bright green ruff, in January.

Eranthis hyemalis is the first to make its bow, but the showier *E. cilicia* and *E. tubergenii* both with larger flowers than the first-named species are only a week or so behind. Left undisturbed, winter aconites will quickly naturalise themselves. The tubers should be planted in August or September.

As the golden chalices of the aconites start to fade, the snowdrops will be pushing up their small green spears, enfolding the delicate looking flower buds. Actually, they are tough and in mild winters will be coming into flower by the end of January to reach the peak of their display by mid-February.

Like the winter aconites, they will soon increase to form large drifts that will continue to bring early promise of spring for many years to come. Best results are obtained from planting while they are still in leaf and specialist suppliers send them out in February for this purpose. Most of us, however, find it easier to plant the dry bulbs in August, although results for the first few seasons may be less satisfactory.

Galanthus nivalis is the common snowdrop, unrivalled in the simplicity of its cool beauty, but for those with a taste for the unusual, there are the outsize flowers of species such as *G. elwesii* with large globular flowers attractively marked with emerald green or *G. nivalis flore pleno* an attractive double form of the common snowdrop.

Following the snowdrops are the brilliant-blue flowers of the *chionodoxas*, aptly called Glory of the Snow. This is another bulbous plant that can be allowed to naturalise itself. Watch out for the tiny grasslike seedlings and leave them undisturbed when the border is being hoed or forked over and you will be rewarded with gleaming pools of blue that make a most impressive sight in March.

Chionodoxa luciliae, whose Cambridge-blue flowers have a distinctive white eye is the species most commonly seen. There are others that are perhaps more eye-catching, including *C. gigantea* with larger gentian-blue flowers and *C. sardensis* which has dark-blue flower buds that open to a vivid royal blue.

The hardy cyclamen produce their dainty shuttlecock flowers all through late winter and early spring. The flowers are preceded by kidney shaped leaves in the previous autumn. Cyclamen do best in a shady situation and make ideal subjects for planting under trees or shrubs. To establish a colony of these delightful plants, a dozen or more corms should be planted, 3in deep, with 6in between the corms. A peaty soil suits them best, but in heavier loamy soils, really generous dressings of peat or leafmould will provide suitable growing conditions.

There are several species of winter-flowering cyclamen, the best known of which is *C. coum*. There are varieties of this with white, deep-rose and pale-pink flowers, all blotched with a deeper cyclamen pink at their throats. The hybrids are particularly worthy of garden space and are obtainable in various shades of pink. Once the corms are established, they will produce a carpet of bloom each year that will bring colour to the darkest days of winter.

C. ibericum flowers later than *C. coum*. The flowers are crimson and the dark-green marbled foliage of this species forms a perfect background. The leaves of *C. repandum*, which is deliciously fragrant, are similarly marked with silver. The flowers of this species open in April and May.

Reverting now to January, the dainty *fleur-de-lis* of *Iris histriodes* will open their delicate-looking buds during the first spell of sunny weather. These are among the best of winter-flowering bulbs and groups give a delightful lift to the front of the border where, if they like you, they will increase and naturalise themselves. The flowers have clear-blue falls and a yellow crest. They will stand up bravely to the worst vagaries of our winter climate. There is a variety known as 'Reine Immaculée' with flowers of a pale saxe blue and a white tongue marked with yellow.

Iris histriodes is followed in February by one of the loveliest of the dwarf bulbous species, *I. danfordiae*. This has flowers of a deep yellow, spotted with grey green at their throats. They are delicately scented. The flowers, like those of the former species, last well, even in bad weather.

At about the same time, or a week or so later, the popular *I. reticulata* will be coming into flower. The bulbs are so inexpensive that one can afford to plant on a lavish scale. The flowers are velvet-textured, of a bluish-purple, deeper in colour at the base and splashed with orange on the falls.

There are, as well, a number of distinctive named varieties of which the best known is probably 'Cantab'. This, as its name suggests, has flowers whose falls are predominantly Cambridge blue flushed with a deeper blue and with an orange tongue. All varieties of *I. reticulata* are sweetly scented. Some, however, are less weather-resistant than the above-mentioned forms.

It is debatable whether or not daffodils should be included in the planting of a herbaceous border. In my opinion, they are bulbs that should be naturalised, either in grass or in the wild garden. I have, however, made one concession in allowing a few drifts of the Tenby daffodil, which grows wild in my neighbourhood, to trespass in a few parts of the border. 'February Gold' is another daffodil that could be used with advantage in a similar manner, as well as one of the real dwarfs such as *Narcissus cyclamineus* or *N. minimus*.

As for tulips, I hold strong views about their proper place in the garden and grow only the earlier flowering species tulips in the border. The Darwins, cottage and May-flowering kinds are much too formal and, unlike the species, cannot be left in the ground to increase.

One of the most striking of these is *Tulipa fosteriana* 'Madame Lefebre' sometimes found listed as 'Red Emperor'. This has long, pointed blooms of a brilliant scarlet. *T. fosteriana* has been crossed with another species, *T. kaufmanniana*, often known as the waterlily tulip, to produce a race of hybrids unrivalled for their colour and beauty. Some inherit the brilliance of the *fosteriana* colouring, others have the best characteristics of the *kaufmannianas* allied to the shapeliness of the flowers of the former. *T. kaufmanniana* itself is a delight to the eye, with crimson-striped ivory petals which shade to gold inside. *Kaufmanniana* and its varieties flower in March, *fosteriana* and its hybrids in early April.

One other group of early-flowering tulips that are well worth a place in the border are *T. greigii* and its hybrids. These are noteworthy, not only for the brilliance of their flower colouring, but also for the decorative effect of their striped leaves, chocolate brown on dark or grey-green.

Among the many worthwhile varieties are 'Ali Baba' and 'Red Riding Hood', both selfs, vermilion and pillarbox red respectively, 'Plaisir', whose petals are striped with carmine and yellow, 'Trinket', with chunky flowers of lemon-yellow and cherry red and 'Segwun' salmon pink and cream.

One of the most impressive spring-flowering bulbs is the Crown Imperial, *Fritillaria imperialis*. A group of these in the border would be sensational in April, when the chaplets of pendent bell-shaped flowers, each with its crown of glossy-green foliage, opens in its full glory. If you can get down to ground level and gaze upwards into the flowers, you will find that each one has a globule of nectar, like a tear, trapped at its centre.

The bulbs and flowers of the crown imperial have a curious, although not entirely unpleasant, foxy aroma. Bulbs are quite expensive to buy, especially the yellows and special named varieties for which you can pay considerable prices. But in good soil, planted to a depth of 6in, they will increase quite rapidly. Overcrowded clumps can be lifted and split up in August, before root action recommences.

In March and April, a whole host of small bulbous plants are available to bring patches of colour to the early spring border. The spring snowflake, *Leucojum vernum,* with green-edged white bells that look like outsize snowdrops, will flower in early March and left undisturbed, in a cool situation, will soon establish sizeable clumps. Bulbs of the spring snowflake should be planted in early autumn, 2-3in deep.

Grape hyacinths, in colours ranging from soft powder blue to deepest cobalt, come into flower at about the same period. 'Heavenly Blue' is one of the finest of these, with miniature hyacinth flowers of bright sky blue. The Oxford and Cambridge muscari, *M. tubergianum,* is another attractive species, so-called because when the flower spikes are fully developed, the top half is a clear Cambridge blue while the lower part is much deeper in colour.

'Blue Pearl' has large spikes of a vivid cobalt blue, while *M. azureum,* which is one of the earliest of the grape hyacinths to come into bloom, has spikes of a delicate Wedgwood blue. There is an attractive white form, *M. botryoides album,*

with fragrant grape-like clusters of pure white flowers. All of
these will thrive in the majority of garden soils, although they
are actually happiest in fairly light sandy soils.

The ornamental squills, with their intensely blue flowers,
that rival the gentians in colouring, look particularly effective
when contrasted with the yellow of daffodils or growing at
the foot of a forsythia. Groups of bulbs can be planted between shrubs and border plants and left to establish themselves which they will do very rapidly if undisturbed.

Scilla bifolia has deep blue flowers shading to a pale colour
at the centre. *S. sibirica* is a deeper shade of blue, with contrasting greenish anthers. 'Spring Beauty', a named variety, is
an improvement on the type with larger flowers and a more
vigorous habit of growth. *S. tubergiana* flowers early with
silver-blue blooms whose petals are faintly lined with a
deeper shade of blue.

Closely related to the scillas is the striped squill, *Pusch-
kinia scilloides*, which is like a miniature hyacinth with
numerous flowers to each spike. These appear in April and
are of a soft pale blue striped with a deeper blue down the
centre of each petal.

The ornamental garlics are a distinct asset to the border in
June. Their rounded heads, packed with tiny florets make a
handsome contrast to the majority of June-flowering perennials. *Allium moly*, whose bulbs are incredibly inexpensive is
still, understandably, the most widely grown species. Its um-
bels of bright yellow flowers are very attractive.

There are, however, other species with much more striking
blooms, such as *A. rosenbachianum* with large globes of lilac-
purple flowers on 3½ft stems and the even larger *A. giganteum*
with violet-tinted pink blooms. My own favourite species is
A. albopilosum which I first saw massed in one of the beds
at Sissinghurst Castle and which I have grown and enjoyed
ever since. This species has enormous spherical heads of pale
purple flowers each flower being surrounded by a silvery

calyx which gives a metallic effect like that of the sea hollies.

The flowers of *A. albopilosum* are the size of a small football and remain very decorative at the seedhead stage. They can then be dried for winter arrangements. Alliums should be planted in September to flower the following summer.

Another useful summer-flowering bulb is *Galtonia candicans*, the summer hyacinth. This is easy to grow in any soil and the bulbs are inexpensive, only a few pence each. The summer hyacinth produces 4ft spikes of white bell-shaped flowers, tinged at their edges with green, in June and July. An added attraction is the broad strap-shaped foliage which is good to look at both before and after the bulbs flower. Summer hyacinth bulbs should be planted 6in deep and the same distance apart from February to April.

The larger gladioli, to my mind, are unsuitable subjects for associating with perennials. They are too artificial in appearance and need careful staking and tying, which makes them look even more out of place in these surroundings. This, however, is not a criticism that can be levelled against the varieties of dwarf gladiolus which are valuable border plants that start to flower in early June and continue over a long period. The corms should be planted in late autumn, 3in deep. In colder districts they must be protected from frost with a covering of peat or weathered ashes.

'Amanda May' is a variety with salmon-pink flowers, flecked with carmine, 'Peach Blossom', one of the loveliest of these dwarf gladioli is rose pink flushed with cream. 'Spitfire' is brick red, blotched with purple and there is also an enchanting white variety, aptly named 'Blushing Bride', since its flowers are flecked with pink and carmine.

Lilies are a decorative feature of any part of the garden, but in the herbaceous border most kinds find the conditions that suit them best, namely, shade at soil level and sunshine for the flowers.

In my herbaceous border, I plant only the easier species

and hybrids, since it is obvious that the plants cannot be given the individual attention they would receive when grown apart from other plants.

Those which are tolerant of a wide range of soil conditions include the regal lily, *Lilium regale*, the orange lily, *L. croceum*, the martagons or Turks' Caps, *L. pardalinum* and the popular tiger lily, *L. tigrinum*. Many of the newer hybrid strains, too, will stand up well to the cavalier treatment they may receive when grown in association with perennials.

It is better to plant lilies towards the front of the border, allowing plenty of space for their full development. In this position, they will be in view at all times and more conveniently placed for maintenance operations such as watering, which they need regularly, tying, staking and spraying.

ANNUALS AND BIENNIALS

In the early days, while a new herbaceous border is becoming established, annuals and biennials can be of value as gap fillers. Annuals such as calendulas, cornflowers, larkspurs, clary, escholtzias and many others will furnish the border with varying colours, shapes and leaf textures that would otherwise be lacking until the basic plantings reach maturity.

There are taller annuals, too, such as the spider flower, *Cleome spinosa* and red mountain spinach, *Atriplex hortensis rubra*, as well as the taller annual sunflowers that make excellent temporary stopgaps at the back of the border while biennials such as sweet williams, Canterbury bells and the stately spires of cultivated foxgloves will fulfil a similar function towards the middle.

Overleaf is a more comprehensive list of hardy and half-hardy annuals that are worth growing in the herbaceous border.

Arctotis	Phlox drummondii
Calliopsis	Poppies
Candytuft	Salpiglossis
Clarkia	Scabious
Dimorpotheca	Stocks
Godetia	Sweet Peas
Lavatera	Sweet Sultan
Linum	Ursinia
Nemesia	Zinnias
Nigella	

Dahlias, too can be very useful, both for filling out the new border and for providing supplementary autumn colour in an established one. The wisest choice is from varieties of medium height since these will need less attention to staking and tying. I avoid the large-flowered decoratives and the giant cactus types. These are excellent for exhibition but less suitable as border plants.

CHAPTER NINE

Methods of Propagation

Stocking a herbaceous border can be a costly operation and any way in which this initial expense can be reduced is worthy of consideration. The cheapest and simplest method of increase is by division, but this, like increase by cuttings or off-shoots has the disadvantage of only increasing plants of the same kind.

Just the same, such plants can be valuable, not only for extending the scope of the border or for in-filling bare patches but also as replacements for diseased or worn-out material. Some perennials, such as lupins and delphiniums are relatively short-lived while others, of which michaelmas daisies are an example, get worn out after a few years through competition among the numerous shoots for nourishment.

Many perennials are easy to raise from seed. Sowings of most kinds can be made outdoors in July to produce plants that will flower the following season. Such plants, however, will not normally reach their full flowering potential until the following year.

Among those perennials that can be raised in this way are achillea, anaphalis, campanula, sea hollies (eryngium), geranium, geum, helenium, hellebore, kniphofia, lupin. oriental poppy and veronica.

Some of the plants from these outdoor sowings of lupins will produce flowers the same autumn. This makes it easy to select the best kinds for growing on in the border. A sowing under glass in spring will give a much larger proportion of autumn-flowering plants.

Other perennials that do best from this latter method are aquilegias, delphiniums and polyanthus.

Another easy way to increase stocks of certain perennials is by means of root cuttings. These consist of portions of root, about 3in long, cut square at the top and sloping at the bottom. The cuttings are inserted in boxes of sandy soil in a cold frame during summer and are ready for planting out the following spring.

In the case of certain perennials, such as phlox, root cuttings have a distinct advantage over other methods of increase. Eeelworm, a serious pest of phlox which can cause considerable damage to the plants, is not transmitted through the roots, so that infested stocks of plants can be replaced by new healthy stock if root cuttings are taken.

Among other perennials that can be increased in this way are anchusas, echinops (globe thistle) gypsophila, oriental poppies and Japanese anemones.

By far the greatest number of perennials, however, are increased by division. This is, in fact, necessary as a regular maintenance operation with plants of rapid spread or those whose clumps deteriorate fairly quickly.

Although most perennials are divided during the winter months, some, including hellebores and the bearded irises, get away better when they are split up as soon as the plants have finished flowering.

Irises need division every third or fourth year. When this is being done, the worn out rhizomes should be discarded. These are the ones at the centre of the clump and are easily recognisable by their shrivelled appearance. The younger, plumper rhizomes at the outer edges of the clumps are the ones that should be used for replanting. They should be severed from the parent clump with a sharp knife and planted out with a 'fan' of leaves to each.

These leaves can be shortened by half before planting to prevent root disturbance by wind while the new plants are getting established. The reason for division so soon after flowering is to give the strong anchoring roots, which spring from the underside of the rhizomes, a chance to get a firm hold in the soil before winter. To accelerate the formation of dense flowering groups, drifts of six to a dozen new rhizomes should be planted.

Some species of hellebore divide more satisfactorily than others. The Christmas rose, *Helleborus niger,* will often sulk for several seasons before developing its full flowering potential anew. The stately *H. corsicus* is even more temperamental and often dies after division. The best way to increase stocks of hellebores is, in fact, from seed, sown as soon as it ripens in June and July.

With the great majority of border plants, however, division is a simple operation. Plants that form a dense mat of fibrous roots can be easily broken up by inserting two garden forks, back to back, in the clumps and levering them apart.

When weeds have invaded the clumps, the soil should be teased out of the roots to facilitate their removal. Where most perennials are concerned, it is better to discard the worn out material at the centres of the clumps and to replant only the younger and more vigorous outside growths.

Some perennials divide best in spring, others get away to a better start if division is carried out in autumn. Among the former are heleniums, day-lilies, hostas, red hot pokers, anaphalis, doronicums, globe thistles, sea hollies, tradescantias, veronicas and the hardy geraniums.

Perennials that flower early are best divided in autumn, while some, like peonies, should never be divided or transplanted unless circumstances, such as the complete overhaul or replanning of a border, make it essential.

CHAPTER TEN

Ground Cover Plants

One of the most interesting developments in recent years is the greatly increased utilisation of ground cover plants to smother weeds and thus cut down maintenance work in perennial, mixed or shrub borders.

For many years, especially in larger gardens, such plants have been widely used as carpeters but it is only recently that their value as weed suppressors has been fully or more widely recognised. Nowadays, practically all nurserymen worthy of the name stock a comprehensive selection of these useful plants, most of which are as decorative as they are useful.

Ground cover plants, however, cannot be expected to perform overnight miracles. In most cases, during their first season or two, weeding between them will still have to be carried out in the usual way. It is not until the plants have closed their ranks to form a close carpet at ground level that their dense mats of leaves and stems can perform their weed-smothering function really effectively.

Choice of ground-cover material can be made from perennials, dwarf creeping shrubs and certain conifers of prostrate habit. Those that are evergreen will provide winter interest.

Some of the more rampant ground coverers need to be treated with a certain amount of caution or they are liable to make a take-over bid for the choicer plants in their immediate vicinity. These, however, can prove especially valuable in the early days of the new border and can then be treated as expendable and be replaced by less rampageous material.

Although we normally think of ivies as climbing plants, they also provide excellent ground cover. Most of the more vigorous species and varieties will rapidly create a close carpet that is capable of suppressing even the most obnoxious weeds. Ivies have the added advantage of thriving in almost any kind of soil or situation and in having no objection to fairly dense shade.

One of the best kinds for this particular purpose is the Irish ivy, *Hedera helix hibernica*. This is a variety of the so-called 'common' ivy whose dark-green glossy foliage will create a complete barrier to all weed growth once the planting becomes established. There are other varieties of the common ivy, such as 'Jubilee', with leaves that are marked with golden yellow and a smaller-leaved form, *H. h. marginata*, whose foliage is a striking medley of creamy white, green and grey.

H. colchica which is sometimes known as the Persian or elephant ivy, has much larger leaves than the former species, up to 6in in length. As well as the green-leaved form there is one with gold-yellow variegation *H.c.* 'Dentata Variegata' and another 'Paddy's Pride' in which the leaves are boldly marked at the centre with yellow that gradually merges, through a pale green to a dark green at the leaf edges. Occasional leaves will be a pure golden yellow in colour.

Cornus canadensis, the creeping dogwood makes an unusual kind of ground cover, forming a dense carpet of green leaves that is emblazoned with white four-petalled flowers in early summer. These are followed by decorative red berries.

For the drier and shadier parts of a border, the rose of Sharon, *Hypericum calycinum* would be hard to better as a ground cover plant. This shrub spreads rapidly by means of underground runners, is practically evergreen and, in July, is smothered in golden chalice-like blooms, like outsize buttercups, but with a handsome central boss of golden stamens.

Periwinkles, too, are easy to establish since they quickly extend their territory by means of the long trailing shoots which root as they run. *Vinca major* the larger-leaved species has vivid-blue trumpet flowers that are produced from April right through to June. There are forms such as *'Variegata'* whose leaves are splashed and margined with cream.

Vinca minor, the lesser periwinkle, has an even greater variety of forms. The leaves and flowers are smaller than those of *V. major* but this species makes a somewhat denser cover. Choice of varieties includes 'Alba' with white flowers; 'Atropurpurea', deep plum-purple; 'Bowles Variety', with flowers of a more intense blue than those of the type; 'Gertrude Jekyll' another worthwhile white and 'Variegata', whose leaves are splashed with creamy-white and which has blue flowers. There are two interesting double varieties, 'Azurea Flore Pleno', with sky-blue flowers and 'Multiplex', whose double blooms are plum-purple.

A less well-known but rampant ground coverer, a member of the borage family, is *Trachystemon orientalis.* This is a handsome plant, with bold hairy leaves that smother the ground beneath them and from which, in early spring, arise branching flower stems with masses of small blue flowers. This would make an ideal subject for planting under large shrubs in the border.

Where shrubs are concerned, however, heathers undoubtedly provide the most effective ground cover of all and are proof against every kind of weed. This is why I like to plant them, in drifts of six to a dozen plants, at intervals along the length of my border. As my soil is faintly alkaline. my plantings are restricted to winter heathers such as *Erica carnea* and *E. darleyensis* which are tolerant of lime.

Most other heather species including the callunas and daboecias are lime-haters, but anyone with neutral or acid soil might well include them in the border plantings, except that, flowering as they do at midsummer and after, they are less valuable than the winter heaths for furnishing interest at an otherwise colour-barren period.

Many popular perennials themselves will provide good ground cover, among them *Anemone hupehensis,* astilbes, bergenias, *Brunnera macrophylla,* epimediums, hellebores, hemerocallis, hostas, *Stachys lanata* and *Tiarella cordifolia.*

One of the best for really rapid cover is a variety of one of our ubiquitous wild plants, bugle or *Ajuga reptans,* to give it its correct botanical name. 'Atropurpurea' is the best garden form. A single plant will cover an area of 3-4sq ft in its first season. The leaves of this variety are a striking beetroot red. The latter make a delightful foil for the blue flower spikes when they appear in May and June. There are also forms with variegated foliage, 'Multicolor' and 'Variegata' whose leaves are mottled with bronze and cream. These do not provide such rapid cover as the purple-leaved variety.

Another group of vigorous cover and smother plants are also related to one of our native wildlings. These are the variegated deadnettles. *Lamium galeobdolon* 'Variegatum' is possibly too much of a good thing for the border of average size but where there is sufficient space for its extensive spread there are few other cover plants that could do the job more efficiently or decoratively, since the foliage is evergreen and marbled with white and silver. each leaf looking as if it has had a quick burst from a spray gun of aluminium paint. In spring, this plant bears spikes of typical yellow deadnettle flowers.

Where space is more restricted, I would prefer to plant one of the less vigorous deadnettle species. One of the best of these is *Lamium maculatum* with emerald-green wrinkled leaves centrally splashed with white and pinkish-purple hooded flowers that appear in May and continue over a long period The only drawback of this otherwise excellent plant is its tendency to seed all over the garden.

This is not a fault, however, of the lovely green-leaved

H

variety *L.m. aureum*. This makes brilliant pools of colour but
has a slower rate of spread than the other two mentioned
above. It is, however, equally effective, within its limits, as
a weed suppressor.

One of the handsomest of the perennials that help us to
win the battle against weeds is the so-called giant saxifrage,
bergenia, which I mentioned in Chapter 3. Their large,
fleshy evergreen leaves hug the soil and suffocate any weed
underneath them. Bergenias have a preference for a partially
shaded situation but will do quite well in the sun provided
they are not kept short of moisture during dry spells.

Once planted, bergenias will need little attention. Division and replanting will need to be undertaken only every
five years or so. Their handsome heads of bloom which, in
some species will be showing colour by mid-February, are a
valuable bonus when there is little else to admire in the border. The best species for ground cover is *B. cordifolia*, with
outsize heart-shaped leaves.

Other perennials which satisfactorily fulfil this weed-
inhibiting function include varieties of hardy geranium, such
as *G. endressi*, the pulmonarias or lungworts, catmint, poly-
gonums and hostas.

Alchemilla mollis, the Lady's mantle, is a ground-cover
plant *par excellence* that associates particularly well with
shrub roses or with grey and silver-leaved plants. The grey-
green foliage covered with a silken-silvery down, is the main
attraction of this old cottage favourite. After a shower of rain,
each leaf will trap a raindrop, like a pearl, at its centre. The
sprays of greenish-yellow flowers do not make a particularly
valuable contribution to the border but are much in demand
by the flower arrangers for use in arrangements featuring
roses.

One of the most decorative of the perennial spurges also
does duty as a ground cover plant. *Euphorbia robbiae* has
dense ground-hugging rosettes of dark green foliage and a

very rapid rate of spread by offshoots. In spring, its stately spires of greenish-yellow bracts are extremely decorative. They open in May and we are still cutting them for the house as I write this in August.

This is also a characteristic of another of the spurges, *E. epithymoides*, whose dense spreading clumps will cover several square feet of ground in a single season and whose massed clusters of lime-green bracts remain decorative for three months or more.

Hostas, with their enormous plantain-like leaves are an obvious choice as weed smotherers. The kinds that do the job best are the giant broad-leaved species and hybrids such as *Hosta sieboldiana*, with blue-grey leaves up to 8in across and *H. fortunei*, a species with leaves of a paler green. The latter is one of the most vigorous of the hostas and a first-rate ground cover plant.

I value *Tellima grandiflora* as much for the beauty of its foliage as for its excellence as a weed suppressor. The rounded hairy leaves are borne in foot-high clumps. They are evergreen and colour to an eye-catching crimson in winter, especially those of the variety *purpurea* which turn an even deeper coppery-purple. The flower spikes, which appear in May, are unusual in appearance, a foot in height and hung with small greenish bells. *Tellima grandiflora* makes a useful cover plant for the shadier parts of the border.

DWARF SHRUBS AS GROUND COVER

Many small shrubs of creeping or prostrate habit also make useful ground cover. An additional advantage of these is that they need less maintenance than the carpeting perennials.

Among those that first come to mind are several species of cotoneaster, such as *C. horizontalis*, the fishbone cotoneaster, which provides dense cover with its flattened herringbone branch structure up to a height of about 3ft.

There are two really prostrate species which will completely close-carpet any area in which they are planted. *C. dammeri,* only a few inches in height is a real ground hugger. It roots as it runs and will eventually cover a very extensive area. *C. conspicua decora,* at 2ft, is taller, and a prostrate version of one of the most popular species of cotoneaster. It can cover an area of 20-30sq ft if allowed to ramble unchecked. Both these shrubs are evergreen with small oval polished leaves and a profusion of scarlet berries in autumn and winter.

Lavender and cotton lavender both make effective cover plants provided they are trimmed back each spring and not allowed to grow too leggy. The old English lavender, *Lavandula spica,* is the strongest grower but more compact varieties such as 'Hidcote' or 'Munstead' are more efficient weed suppressors.

PROSTRATE CONIFERS

There are several prostrate conifers that will spread their branches, densely clad with foliage, over the soil to perform this all-important function of weed suppression.

These are found mainly among the ranks of the junipers and include such forms as *Juniperus media pfitzeriana* with long branches of grey-green feathery foliage growing horizontally, *J. sabina tamariscifolia* a semi-miniature juniper suitable for planting at the front of the border and *J. conferta* a bright-green prostrate species and one of the best for ground cover. *J. horizontalis* 'Bar Harbour' is a flat North American form with a mat of soft grey-green foliage that colours to an interesting purple in winter.

CHAPTER ELEVEN

Planning Different Borders

A herbaceous or mixed border should not be planned in a hit or miss fashion. The placing of the plants needs a good deal of preliminary consideration and colour groupings play an important part. More important still is the relation between the size of each group of plants and the overall dimensions of the border. Where very small borders are concerned, it may be possible to achieve a satisfactory effect with single plants of each kind for the middle and back positions with up to three in a group of the smaller edging plants.

In a border of this kind, the use of shrubs for interplanting would be inadvisable. If any are included, they should be real midgets such as *Genista hispanica* or *Berberis stenophylla* 'Corallina Compacta'. The whole of the planting, in fact, should be scaled down to suit the restricted area involved.

Where more space is available, the best effects are obtained by planting in comparatively large groups. Regularity should be avoided and each drift of plants should merge imperceptibly into the next with no hint of regimentation. For this reason, it may be necessary to allow some frontal groups to drift back into the middle border while the occasional tall plant, or group of plants can be brought forward to provide a focal point of interest. This works particularly well with subjects such as delphiniums or the foxtail lilies whose tall spires of bloom are shown off to best advantage in this kind of position.

For the majority of borders, groups of three plants will be sufficient for the background and middle. At the edge, where smaller shrubs and perennials are used, groups of six or more plants may be needed to create the required effect.

In the accompanying plans, the number of plants per group have purposely been omitted. This enables them to be adapted to the large or small border by varying the numbers used.

1 PLAN FOR BORDER WITH HEDGE AS BACKGROUND USING ONLY HERBACEOUS PERENNIALS

Achillea filipendulina 'Gold Plate' · Anaphalis yedoensis · Nepeta mussini · Delphinium Belladonna 'Lamartine' · Michaelmas Daisy 'Crimson Brocade' · Alchemilla mollis · Michaelmas Daisy 'Harrington's Pink' · Eryngium alpinum 'Amethyst' · Kniphofia 'Maid of Orleans' · Iris 'Party Dress' · Artemisia lactiflora · Macleya cordata · Helianthus 'Loddon Gold' · Papaver orientale 'Mrs Perry' · Sidalcea 'Mrs Alderson' · Campanula lactiflora 'Loddon Anna' · Penstemon 'Firebird' · Echinops ritro · Chrysanthemum maximum 'Esther Read' · Monarda didyma 'Croftway Pink' · Delphinium 'Pink Sensation' · Acanthus mollis · Russell Lupins · Thalictrum dipterocarpum · Phlox 'Mia Ruys' · Doronicum 'Harpur Crewe' · Heucherella 'Bridget Bloom' · Ajuga reptans 'Variegata' · Tiarella cordifolia

2 PLAN FOR MIXED BORDER OF SHRUBS AND PERENNIALS FOR A MAINLY SUMMER DISPLAY

Cotoneaster lacteus · Stachys lanata · Helenium 'The Bishop' · Eryngium planum · Symphytum peregrinum · Cytisus praecox · Pyrus salicifolia 'Pendula' · Philadelphus 'Belle Etoile' · Rose 'Mme Pierre Ogar' · Euphorbia epithymoides · Helleborus corsicus · Solidago 'Golden Wings' · Artemisia absynthium 'Lambrook Silver' · Verbascum broussa · Romneya x trichocalyx · Hemerocallis 'Ballet Dancer' · Hosta sieboldiana glauca · Rose 'Constance Spry' · Echinacea 'The King' · Ceratostigma willmottianum · Hamamelis mollis · Spiraea 'Anthony Waterer' · Salvia officinalis 'Tricolor' · Buddleia davidii 'Royal Red' · Cimicifuga ramosa · Berberis thunbergii 'Red Pillar' · Euphorbia characias · Prunus sargentii · Lavatera olbia rosea · Kniphofia 'Royal Standard' · Dicentra spectabilis · Caryopteris x clandonensis 'Ferndown' · Solidago 'Lemore' · Epimedium 'Rose Queen' · Erigeron 'Charity'

3. PLAN FOR A 'BLUE' BORDER

Eryngium tripartitum · Brunnera macrophylla · Penstemon hetrophyllus 'Blue Gem' · Polyanthus 'Blue Strain' · Echinops ritro 'Blue Ball' · Cynoglossum nervosum · Michaelmas Daisy 'Ada Ballard' · Pulsatilla vulgaris · Anchusa 'Morning Glory' · Baptisia australis · Agapanthus 'Headbourne Hybrids' · Salvia haematodes · Rosemary 'Miss Jessup's Upright' · Salvia superba · Lavender 'Munstead Blue' · Rura graveolens 'Jackman's Blue' · Aconitum wilsonii 'Barker's Variety' · Delphinium 'Blue Riband' · Symphitum caucasicum · Campanula glomerata dahurica · Hebe 'Autumn Beauty' · Michaelmas Daisy 'Harrison's Blue' · Phlox 'Bleu de Pervenche' · Aconitum 'Bressingham Spire' · Platycodon grandiflorum · Hibiscus syriacus 'Blue Bird' · Campaula persicifolia · Caryopteris clandonensis · Linum perenne · Ceanothus 'Gloire de Versailles' · Salvia uliginosa · Lupin 'Thunder-cloud' · Physostegia virginiana 'Vivid' · Gentiana septemfida · Nepeta mussinii 'Six Hills Giant' · Perovskia atriplicifolia · Pulmonaria 'Munstead Blue'

4. PLAN FOR A WHITE AND SILVER BORDER

Hibiscus syriacus 'W.R.Smith' · Artemisia 'Silver Queen' · Magnolia stellata · Hydrangea paniculata 'Grandiflora' · Senecio laxifolius · Paeony 'Kelway's Glorious' · Lilac (Syringa) 'Mme.Lemoine' · Phlomis fruticosa · Phlox 'Mia Ruys' · Campanula carpatica 'Alba' · Pyrus salicifolia pendula · Anaphalis yedoensis · Anemone x hybrida 'Louise Uhink' · Primula denticulata 'Alba' · Spiraea arguta · Cimicifuga cordifolia · Michaelmas Daisy 'Blandie' · Campanula persicifolia alba · Lavandula vera 'Alba' · Buddleia davidii 'White Profusion' · Chrysanthemum maximum 'Horace Read' · Artemesia 'Lambrook Silver' · Aruncus silvester · Rosmarinus officinalis · Philadelphus 'Manteau d'Hermine' · Convolvulus cneorum · Helichrysum serotinum · Dianthus 'White Ladies' · Astilbe 'Irrlicht'

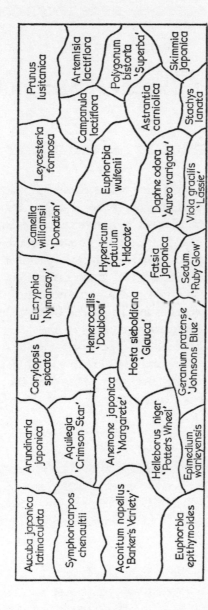

The plant layout within the border includes:

Aucuba japonica latimaculata | Arundinaria japonica | Corylopsis spicata | Eucryphia 'Nymansay' | Camellia williamsii 'Donation' | Leycesteria formosa | Prunus lusitanica

Symphoricarpos chenaultii | Aquilegia 'Crimson Star' | Hemerocallis 'Doubloon' | Hypericum patulum 'Hidcote' | Euphorbia wulfenii | Campanula lactiflora | Artemisia lactiflora

Aconitum napellus 'Barker's Variety' | Anemone japonica 'Margarete' | Hosta sieboldiana 'Glauca' | Fatsia japonica | Daphne odora 'Aureo varigata' | Astrantia carniolica | Polygonum bistorta 'Superba'

Helleborus niger 'Potter's Wheel' | Geranium pratense 'Johnsons Blue' | Sedum 'Ruby Glow' | Viola gracilis 'Lassie' | Stachys lanata | Skimmia japonica

Euphorbia epithymoides | Epimedium warleyensis

5 PLAN FOR A BORDER IN PARTIAL SHADE

CHAPTER TWELVE

Other Border Subjects

Although nobody, with the wide choice of plant material already mentioned, should ever be at a loss for a sufficient variety of plants to furnish a herbaceous border, there are other kinds that can be used to enhance its interest, particularly for the plantsman or garden specialist. These include bamboos and ornamental grasses, together with hardy ferns. The last named can prove extremely useful where the border or some parts of it are in partial or complete shade.

Bamboos themselves are members of the grass or *graminacae* family and the dense thickets of leaves and stems that most of them produce make them invaluable subjects for screen and background planting. Many of the species are either shade lovers or shade tolerant. All of them flourish best in moist soil conditions.

One of the disadvantages, where the more popular species are concerned, is their invasive tendencies. They spread rapidly by means of underground stolons and the more vigorous kinds have a way of smothering any choicer plants in their immediate vicinity, if left to grow unchecked. The answer, however, is to keep a close watch on the clumps and to chop back any suckers with a sharp spade before they overstep their allotted areas.

The best time to plant bamboos is in early autumn or late spring. Transplanting during the winter months sometimes results in losses. But don't despair if newly-planted specimens go for weeks or even months without displaying any signs of life. Plants will often remain dormant until midsummer before they condescend to unfurl their new season's growths.

The two main groups from which most species of garden bamboos are drawn are Arundinaria and Phyllostachys. The former includes many of the most popular and best known species, including those formerly listed under the generic heading 'Bambusa'.

Arundinaria nitida is one of the most elegant and majestic of these with purple-flushed canes 10-11ft in height and with masses of willowlike foliage. Another tall-growing species is the Metake, *A. japonica*, which is cultivated commercially in some parts of the British Isles for its canes.

Clumps of this bamboo in the garden can provide useful supplies of garden canes up to 6ft tall. They may not have the same lasting qualities as the commercial article, but a fresh supply becomes available each succeeding year. The canes of *A. japonica* are olive-green colour with wiry side shoots bearing a profusion of glossy dark-green leaves.

There are several smaller species of arundinaria suitable for the edge or middle of the border. One of the most useful of these is *A. pumila*, with purple canes whose compact habit makes it a good carpeter. This has an extensive spread and will provide excellent ground cover. Another with similar useful and decorative qualities is *A. pygmaea*. This species is noteworthy for its fine leaves, up to 5in long and an inch in width.

A. veitchii (syn *Sasa veitchii*), is a small dense-growing species that forms close thickets of purple canes 3-4ft in height. The oval leaves die off at their margins in winter to provide a decorative variegated appearance.

The bamboos in the phyllostachys group have, in general, less invasive tendencies than those mentioned above. For this reason, they are more suited for the present day gardens of small to medium size. The black bamboo, *Phyllostachys nigra*, is so-called because its stems, green at first, turn a striking jet black when they reach maturity in their second season.

Named varieties include 'Boryana', whose arching stems are generously furnished with leaves, 'Henonis', which is similar in character and 'Punctata', which resembles *P. nigra* itself.

Incidentally, it is interesting to note that the young shoots of *P. nigra* and its varieties are edible and, as anyone with a knowledge of Chinese cooking will confirm, something of a delicacy.

ORNAMENTAL GRASSES

Clumps of the ornamental grasses, dotted here and there in the border, can add considerably to the interest of a mixed planting of shrubs and perennials. There are both annual and perennial kinds and their tufts and hummocks of narrow leaves make an effective contrast to the more rounded silhouettes of many other border plants. Many provide colour contrast as well in the shape of blue-grey, silver, cream or variegated foliage.

The fescues, grasses of such great value in the composition of lawn seed mixtures, also include some ornamental species which make dense clumps of colourful foliage less than a foot in height and ideally suited for planting at the edge of the border.

Festuca ovina glauca, often known as the 'Blue Grass', has dainty silver-blue foliage. *F. punctoria,* with spine-tipped leaves of greyish green, is no less attractive. Both make ideal plants for grouping at the front of the border.

Some of the loveliest of the ornamental grasses are found in the genus Miscanthus, some species of which are still sometimes found listed under the generic title of Eulalia. They are tall and elegant, growing up to 6ft tall. This makes them an excellent choice for back-row planting. Clumps can also be brought forward to provide focal points of interest. Although none of the miscanthus species is evergreen, the dead leaves and stems, cinnamon in colour, retain their interest well into the New Year until the winter gales leave only a few tattered remnants.

Miscanthus sacchariflorus will reach heights of 10ft or more but is somewhat too rampageous for the average-sized border. It does, however, provide a first-class windbreak for borders in exposed situations. The variety 'Aureus', with gold-striped leaves is shorter and less vigorous. This is well worth growing.

It is, however, *M. sinensis* and its varieties that provides the choicest material for border planting. I like to see clumps of one or other of these superb grasses planted at irregular intervals along the entire length. *M. sinensis* itself has a striking white central stripe to each of its leaves. It grows 6ft tall. 'Gracillimus' has narrower leaves and a more arching habit of growth; the leaves of 'Variegatus' and 'Zebrinus' are marked with cream and gold respectively, the former lengthwise, the latter barred transversely. All these varieties grow to around the 5ft mark and are sufficiently vigorous to form bold hummocks of foliage in a single season.

The bent grasses form another vital constituent of the more hardwearing lawn seed mixtures. It is these which produce those long wiry flower stalks that defy every assault of the mower and make back-breaking hand clipping necessary during their flowering season.

The ornamental varieties, however, are beyond criticism. Two of the best known are annuals, Cloud Grass, *Agrostis nebulosa* and *A. pulchella* and are much prized as dried ingredients of winter flower arrangements. *A setacea*, the Bristle Bent, is an unusual species, native to Britain. It forms small cushions of fine glaucous foliage.

In addition to those already mentioned, there are several eye-catching striped grasses of which the Ribbon Grass, *Phalaris arundinacea* 'Picta', sometimes called 'Gardeners'

Garters' is the kind most commonly seen. Everyone should find room for one or more clumps of this colourful grass, gaily striped with green and cream. It grows 3-4ft tall. Others, equally worth growing but less often seen include a yellow-striped form of the Meadow Foxtail, *Alopecurus pratensis* 'Foliis Variegatis' and *Molina coerulea* 'Variegata' whose leaves are edged with cream.

Bowles Golden Grass, *Millium effusum,* is a delightful variety of our native wood millet that forms compact golden cushions. The Wood Rush, *Luzula sylvatica,* which grows wild in many parts of the country, has an attractive form 'Marginata', whose leaves are banded with ivory-white at their edges.

But the stateliest and most impressive of all the ornamental grasses is the Pampas Grass, *Cortaderia selloana,* which forms magnificent clumps up to 8ft in height with a spread of similar dimensions. Pampas grass can be rather overpowering for the smaller garden but nothing could be more effective where a bold effect is being aimed at.

As well as the ordinary form, with its outsized silver-grey plumes and the silver-pink variety, 'Rendatleri', there is another that is much more compact not exceeding 5ft in height. This has rounded plumes on 4-5ft stems and is called 'Pumila'. Spring planting is recommended and the crowns of the plants should not be more than $2\frac{1}{2}$in below the surface of the soil.

Many of the ornamental grasses can be raised easily from seed, especially annual species such as cloud grass, quaking grass and the Foxtail Millet. Others, equally easy to propagate from spring sowings outdoors *in situ* are the Squirrel-tail Grass, *Hordeum jubatum,* with silky barley-like tassels and *Lagurus ovatus,* the Harestail Grass, with soft fluffy plumes that give it its popular name.

HARDY FERNS

For areas of a border in full or partial shade, hardy ferns are invaluable as in-fillers between shade-loving or shade-tolerant shrubs and perennials. The choice of hardy ferns is wide and anyone whose experience of these useful plants is limited to the harts-tongue and male ferns of our woods and hedgerows is in for a pleasant surprise when he grows them.

These hardy species and varieties of fern ask for nothing special in the way of cultivation apart from a soil that is sufficiently moist at all times. They can be very effective, planted in association with hostas, hellebores, astilbes or bulbs such as narcissus and snowdrops.

Some will flourish in full sunlight, but in this situation a moist cool rootrun is of special importance. Those which do include the Male Fern, *Dryopteris filix-mas*, the Hard Shield Fern, *Polystichum aculeatum* and the Hart's Tongue, *Phyllitis scolopendrium*. All of these, however, would be happier in conditions of partial shade.

Maidenhair ferns are delightful, but many species are on the tender side and need the protection of a cool greenhouse. The hardiest is *Adiantum pedatum* with feathery fronds that make this the daintiest of all the hardy ferns. Two others suited to sheltered positions outside are *A. capillus-veneris* and *A. venustum*.

The spleenworts are another race of comparatively dwarf ferns, but these are completely hardy and can be found growing wild on walls and rock banks in all parts of the country. *Asplenium adiantum nigrum*, the Black Spleenwort, has triangulated leaves, dark green on their upper surfaces and cinnamon brown on the reverse. Two others equally ubiquitous in the wild are the Wall Rue, *A. ruta muraria* and the Maidenhair Spleenwort, *A. trichomanes*. Any of these could provide a decorative addition to a shady border that is edged with paving or retaining brick or stone.

One of my favourite hardy ferns is *Blechnum tabulare,* portions of which have been transported from garden to garden during my frequent house moves. This is a fern with ladder-like foliage, evergreen, with handsome dark-green leathery fronds, 2ft tall and transversely divided into narrow sections.

Another delightful species, as full of grace as the plumes of the bird whose name it bears is *Matteuccia struthopteris,* the Ostrich Fern. Planted in a moist and shady situation, it will reward you with the lovely curving fronds that are so suggestive of its popular name.

Most handsome of all, and a striking subject for the back of a moist shady border is the Royal Fern, *Osmunda regalis,* which is found in the wild in marshy areas in some parts of the British Isles. It is, however, becoming so increasingly rare that it has now been placed on the list of protected wild plants.

This is a truly magnificent fern, as regal as its name implies. It forms very large clumps of enormous leaves, 6ft or more in height.

CHAPTER THIRTEEN

Pests and Diseases

This chapter is, of necessity, a short one since fortunately the majority of herbaceous perennials suffer from remarkably few pests and diseases. There are always the usual ones that plague most gardeners such as slugs and snails, caterpillars and aphids. These can be dealt with in the appropriate manner as also can outbreaks of fungus disease such as powdery mildew, which attacks several border plants and, in particular, michaelmas daisies.

This last named perennial is susceptible also to a virus disease, *Verticullium vilmorinii* or wilt disease. This is especially prevalent in wet summers. It starts in the roots and lower stems, turning the leaves yellow and eventually brown and dead-looking. The flowers, when they open, are stunted and badly wilted. Affected plants should be removed and burnt.

Fresh stocks of healthy plants can be obtained from cuttings taken from the tips of new young growths. At this stage they are seldom, if ever infected by the disease. Once established, these new plants should go back in a different part of the border to avoid reinfection.

Powdery mildew should be treated as soon as the first signs of the disease appear. Affected plants should be dusted with sulphur or sprayed with a suitable fungicide. As well as michaelmas daisies, delphiniums are particularly susceptible to this unsightly fungus disease.

J

Bearded iris are subject to leaf spot and iris rust. Neither of these diseases need prove particularly troublesome if the old leaves are cut down and burnt when the border is having its autumn tidying-up.

Eelworms are minute, transparent eel-like worms, too small to be seen by the naked eye, that attack a number of border plants, including phlox and chrysanthemums. In the case of phlox, their activities are confined to the leaves and stems of the plants. Root cuttings, therefore, obtained in the manner described in Chapter 10, will produce new stocks of healthy plants.

Most other border pests can be effectively dealt with by the regular use of the appropriate insecticides or fungicides in dust or spray form. A fairly recent introduction is the systemic insecticide which is absorbed into the sap of the treated plants, rendering it lethal to sap-sucking insects such as aphides and others over a period of a week or more. This does away with the need for repeat spraying after a day or so to kill off newly emerged young.

Although DDT is no longer available for the amateur gardener's use, there are newer chemicals, equally effective, but non-toxic to human, animal and bird life.

One of the best safeguards against severe attacks from garden pests and diseases is good cultivation. Healthy plants offer a far greater resistance than weak, sickly ones to the majority of these. A well-balanced feeding programme that includes adequate supplies of humus-rich material is of great importance.

Where animal manure is unobtainable, the compost heap can provide an effective substitute. Properly made and ripened, compost will supply the full needs of almost all garden plants, including the vital trace elements so necessary to plant health and vigour.

A badly kept, untidy garden acts as a harbourage for a host of pests and diseases. Slugs and snails multiply in long grass

and weeds while other pests proliferate in untidy hedge bottoms. Diseased plant remains should never be left lying about or even be consigned to the compost heap. They should go on the bonfire without delay.

Even with all the short cuts to ease of maintenance and cultivation the job of keeping up a herbaceous or mixed border in the manner that it deserves is not going to be a sinecure. But it is a worthwhile and rewarding task and one that will give ever-increasing pleasure as this attractive garden feature comes to maturity.

Index